CW00554342

WALES
A WALK THROUGH TIME

HARLECH TO CEMAES BAY

BRIAN E. DAVIES

AMBERLEY PUBLISHING

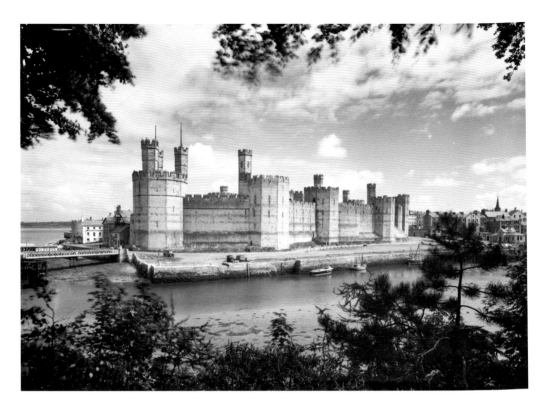

Caernarfon Castle, 1953.

To Meg, Cari, Beth, Seren and Ieuan.

First published 2014

Amberley Publishing
The Hill, Stroud, Gloucestershire, GL5 4EP
www.amberley-books.com

Copyright © Brian E. Davies, 2014

The right of Brian E. Davies to be identified as the
Author of this work has been asserted in accordance with
the Copyrights, Designs and Patents Act 1988.

ISBN 978 1 84868 709 7

All rights reserved. No part of this book may be reprinted
or reproduced or utilised in any form or by any electronic,
mechanical or other means, now known or hereafter
invented, including photocopying and recording, or in
any information storage or retrieval system, without the
permission in writing from the Publishers.

British Library Cataloguing in Publication Data.
A catalogue record for this book is available from the
British Library.

Typesetting by Amberley Publishing.
Printed in Great Britain.

Contents

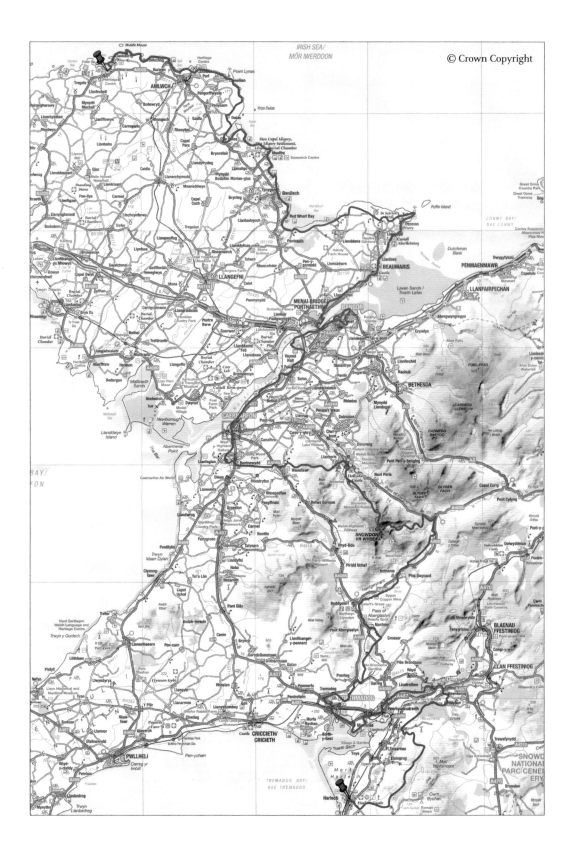

© Crown Copyright

Acknowledgements

I'd like to thank Bill Kenny for his company on Snowdon, Pat Ward for his photographic help and all those who contributed images and information, including National Museums of Wales, National Library of Wales, Cadw (The Welsh Government's Historic Environment Service), Snowdonia National Park Authority, Royal Commission on the Ancient and Historical Monuments of Wales, Gwynedd Council, Gwynedd Archives, Gwynedd Museum & Art Gallery, National Trust, Visit Wales, Ffestiniog & Welsh Highland Railways, Magnox Trawsfynydd, Electric Mountain, Sail Loft & Copper Kingdom Centres, Bangor Civic Society, Sioned Jones (Anglesey Council Coastal Access Officer), Wales Coast Path officers, Molly Lovatt (Natural Resources Wales), Dave Newbould (Origins), Robin Llywelyn (Portmeirion), Martin Pritchard, Archie Harris (Talsarnau Times), Timm Masterson (Vintage Anglesey Prints), Dr Ronald Austin, E. W. Thomas & the late H. G. Williams, Glaslyn Osprey Project, Dewi Owen, Euryn Williams and Kathleen & Robert Williams.

Publications referred to include: *Gerald of Wales* (trans. Lewis Thorpe), *Wild Wales* (George Borrow), *Harlech Castle, Caernarfon Castle, Beaumaris Castle* (Arnold Taylor), *The Isle of Anglesey Coastal Path Official Guide* (Carl Rogers), *Illustrated London News* and local signboards and guides including those for Porthmadog, Llanberis, Caernarfon, Bangor, Beaumaris, Moelfre, Amlwch, Bull Bay and Cemaes Bay.

The internet has been invaluable, particularly Wikimedia Commons (Sources: Bonhams, Los Angeles County Museum of Art, State Library of Queensland and Authors: Oosoom, Herbert Ortner, Velela, Robin Leicester), People's Collection Wales, Wrecksite and many local community and history websites.

Ordnance Survey Maps reproduced: © Crown Copyright. All rights reserved. Licence number 100050463.

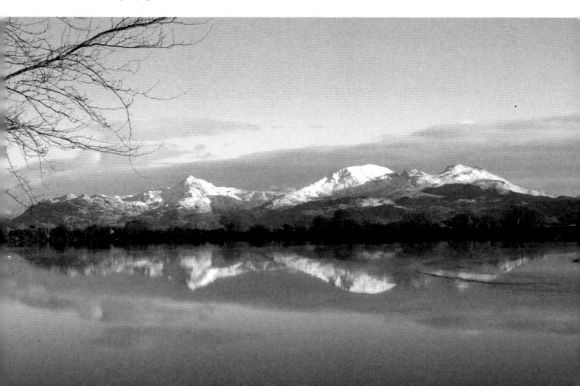

Introduction

On 29 May 1953, Hillary and Tenzing set foot on the summit of Mount Everest, becoming the first climbers to ascend the world's highest mountain. The proprietor of the Pen-y-Gwryd Hotel in Snowdonia was one of the first to receive the news and he woke all his guests in the middle of the night and opened the champagne. The great peak, named after a Welshman, had finally been conquered! Members of the Everest team, led by Sir John Hunt, had based themselves at the Pen-y-Gwryd Hotel during their training for the expedition, finding winter conditions in Snowdonia perfect for their preparation. The famous hotel is one of the stopping-off points on our walk through Wales and provides an ideal starting point for our own more modest climb of Snowdon.

Our 120-mile walk through the mountains and around the coastline of North Wales has history at every step, with stories of triumph and disaster in equal measure. One of the triumphs was Telford's great suspension bridge over the Menai Strait, completed in 1826, and we'll have the pleasure of crossing it to reach Ynys Môn. Anglesey's rugged coast has seen many disastrous shipwrecks, including the tragic sinking of the *Royal Charter* in 1859, with the loss of over 400 lives, as well as millions of pounds worth of gold. We'll recall these events and explore many fascinating places along our way.

The walk from Harlech to Cemaes Bay is the third and final part of a journey of some 370 miles from the southernmost to the northernmost point in Wales. I've chosen the route and accompanying images to showcase the outstanding landscape and history of Wales and each chapter describes an attractive section of the journey. Most sections can be walked in a day while the longer sections can be divided if so wished. The walk starts at the magnificent castle of Harlech and follows the Ardudwy Way through the Rhinogydd, continuing around the Dwyryd estuary to the magical village of Portmeirion. We cross the Cob causeway to Porthmadog and visit the spectacular Aberglaslyn Pass and Nantgwynant before ascending Snowdon. We continue from Llanberis to historic Caernarfon then follow the Menai to the city of Bangor. On Anglesey, we follow the beautiful Coastal Path around to Cemaes Bay and at the end there's a little boat trip to Middle Mouse island, the northernmost point in Wales.

The 1:50,000 scale 'Landranger' OS maps included and directions in the text will enable the walker to follow the route without difficulty. More detailed 'Explorer' maps are a useful additional aid and the Anglesey Coastal Path Official Guide is also recommended. The route crosses some high and exposed ground and weather conditions can change very quickly so it's important that proper clothing and equipment are used. Adequate supplies of food and drink should be carried and maps, compass and whistle are always essentials.

I've featured some of the welcoming hostelries I found along the route and these are well-placed to provide rest and refreshment for the weary traveller. Enjoy the walk!

Brian E. Davies
1 March 2014

Chapter One
Harlech to Maentwrog
14.0 miles (22.6 km)

A Bronze Age 'Crown of Thorns'

The first day of our long journey starts at Harlech Castle and follows a fairly strenuous, exposed upland route that includes nearly 1,900 feet of ascent and takes us to the foothills of the Rhinog mountains. We follow the northern section of the Ardudwy Way and pass a number of prehistoric sites including the spectacular Bronze Age stone circle of Bryn Cader Faner. The Way crosses the geological formation of Cambrian rocks of the Harlech Dome and there are wonderful mountain and coastal views to enjoy before we descend to the lake of Llyn Tecwyn Isaf. We then ascend past the little church of Llandecwyn to the upper lake of Llyn Tecwyn Uchaf, and join a section of the Wales Coast Path, which is currently routed around Maentwrog due to the rebuilding of the Pont Briwet bridge. The Path passes through Coed Felinrhyd woodland, dropping down to Maentwrog hydroelectric station before climbing again and then descending to Maentwrog, a village that once housed workers from the local slate mines.

The walk begins at the famed castle of Harlech, with its commanding views of the Snowdonia mountains, which seem to beckon us forward. The great castle has inspired many artists over the centuries and its place in the landscape is charmingly captured in the watercolour (*below*) by Anthony Vandyke Copley Fielding (1787–1855).

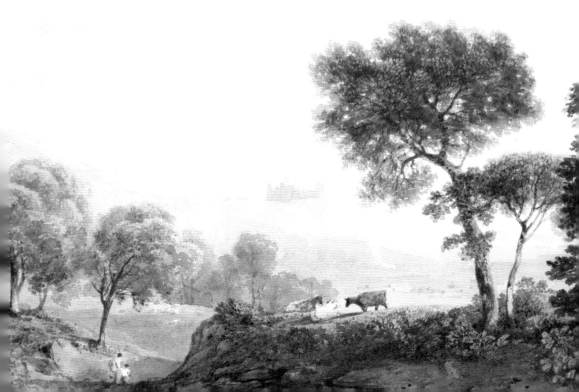

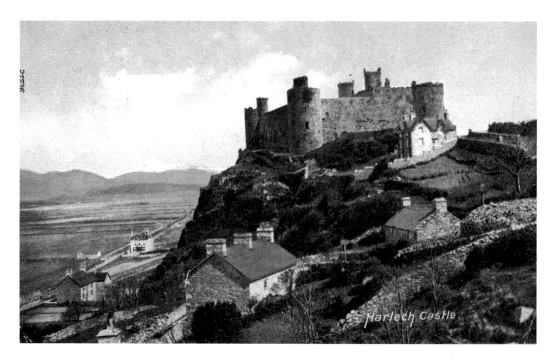

Harlech Castle's spectacular presence on the great rock overlooking the coastal marsh of Morfa Harlech has changed little since the photograph above was taken around a century ago. The castle fortunately survived orders to destroy it after it fell to Parliamentarian forces in 1647, marking the end of the Civil War. It was the Royalists' last stronghold just as it had been the last Lancastrian stronghold, besieged and taken by Yorkist forces during the Wars of the Roses, an event famously remembered in song. It had previously secured its place in Welsh history when it was captured in 1404 by Owain Glyndŵr during his great rebellion. Glyndŵr held court there until 1409, when the castle was retaken for the English by Harry of Monmouth, the future King Henry V.

The view below of Harlech Castle with Snowdon behind it remains one of the most enduring images of Wales.

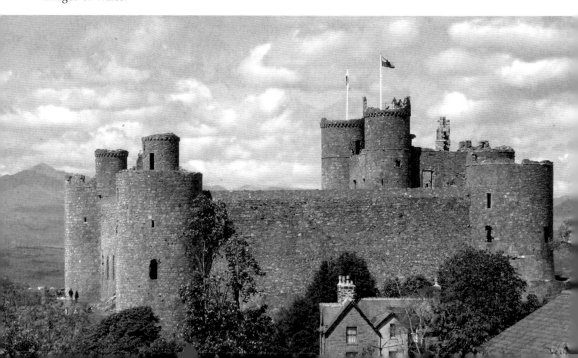

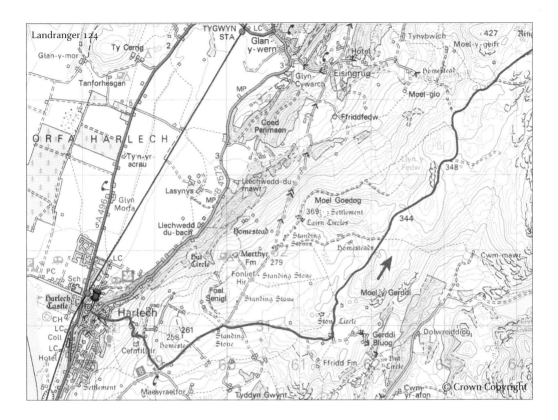

Harlech Castle was begun by Edward I in 1283 following the wars against Prince Llywelyn and is a World Heritage listed site, along with Conwy, Caernarfon and Beaumaris castles. The latter two castles will be visited later in the walk but a tour of Harlech Castle before starting is highly recommended – the view from the ramparts is quite breathtaking!

The walk starts from the castle square and goes steeply uphill, across the crossroads and past the Lion Hotel, continuing uphill along Pen Dref. After about a mile, a crossroads is reached near a former chapel, where the route turns left. In another half a mile or so, it forks right along the lane signposted with the Ardudwy Way sign (there's a standing stone on the right, just before the fork). A mile further along this gated lane, the route reaches the signposts of the Ardudwy Way proper, where a left turn is taken to follow its northern section. The Way is well waymarked with the distinctive black buzzard on a yellow background. The trail passes to the left of Rhyd yr Eirin, crossing numerous ladder stiles and continues across high, exposed moorland, with waymarkers on the stiles and gates showing the route. There's a magnificent view of Morfa Harlech and the Dwyryd Estuary to the left and an equally impressive view of the Rhinog mountains to the right. After about 3 miles, and about 200 metres after a final gate and ladder stile, the Way goes left, as signposted, leaving the main track. The path is easy to miss here; the first, short bit is closer to the wall than it first appears. Soon, a clear, straight track is reached, heading north-east. This is an ancient Bronze Age trackway dating back some 3,000–4,000 years.

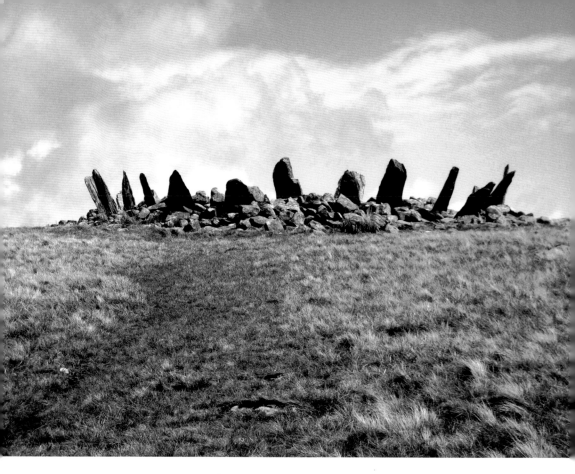

In just under a mile, the Bronze Age trackway leads to the iconic Bryn Cader Faner burial site, which soon appears on the hill ahead – it's quite a sight, with the mountains of Snowdonia in the background. Where the Ardudwy Way turns off left, a detour of about 150 metres to the north-east leads up to the knoll where the spectacular Bronze Age cairn stands. The photograph above was taken from the south-west, approaching the site.

The monument is a 'cairn circle' comprising a burial mound and a stone circle, some 8.5 metres across. The outward jagged stone pillars, leaning at an angle, have been aptly described as a 'crown of thorns'. There were apparently thirty stone pillars originally but a number have been removed, possibly by early tomb raiders or, more bizarrely, by the Army during manoeuvres before or during the Second World War. The idea that the monument could have been used as a gunnery target beggars belief! There seem to be about twenty-four stones of varying sizes still standing – the missing ones were removed mainly from the east side. The cairn is thought to date from the late third millennium BC and it's remarkable that the monument has survived largely intact for so many centuries. The stone circle's dramatic position and its remote location add to its wonder and mystery and Bryn Cader Faner is unquestionably one of the most striking Bronze Age sites in the United Kingdom. It certainly rewards the long walk to view it.

Returning to the Ardudwy Way where it turns left, we follow the track down with great views of Snowdon ahead as we descend.

As we follow the marker posts down and across a boggy area, the Traeth Bach estuary comes into view with the island of Ynys Gifftan and Portmeirion village behind it. Portmeirion was famously created by Sir Clough Williams-Ellis and will be explored in the next chapter.

The path passes through a gate and through wall gaps, eventually becoming a grassy track, which bends around right. It passes through another gate and follows the left-hand field edge down to the lane. The sign here directs us left along the lane and through the farmyard of Caerwych, which has a riding centre. The lane winds steeply downwards, around several hairpin bends, and it's very pleasant to be in woodland after crossing the high moorland. The route passes through a gate onto a further lane, continuing ahead, and a left turn at the next T-junction leads to the charming little lake of Llyn Tecwyn Isaf (*below*).

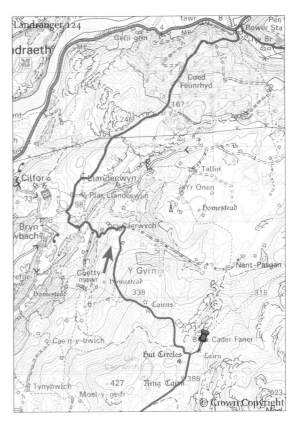

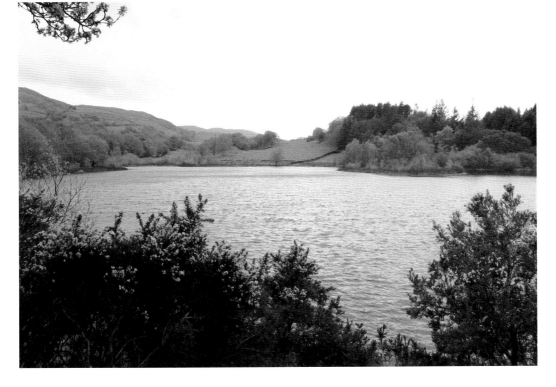

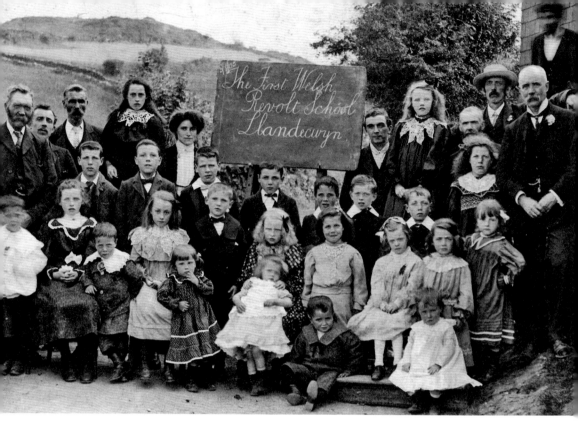

At the lake, the ongoing route turns sharply right up the hill, but just a short distance along the lane to the left is the old Bron-Tecwyn Wesleyan Methodist chapel, which was the unlikely setting for a school revolt in 1906. The first Welsh 'Revolt School' (*above*) was set up in the chapel vestry in response to the Balfour Education Act of 1902, which transferred responsibility for financing all schools, including Anglican Church schools, to the local authority. This was unpopular in Nonconformist rural Wales and Merionethshire County Council was basically unwilling to pay for Anglican education 'on the rates'. The religious revivals of the time probably accentuated people's feelings.

The National school at Llandecwyn, just opposite the chapel, was run by the Church and in 1905 the council tried to close it to coerce pupils to attend the Council School instead.

The issue caused heated debate in government circles, with Lloyd George very much at the fore. An inquiry was ordered into the Llandecwyn case and, even though the inquiry concluded that a school was not needed in Llandecwyn, the National School was allowed to continue. The council was not prepared to give in and decided to open a new school, which became known as the 'Revolt School', to compete against the National School. The council clearly won the argument as, by August 1906, their 'Revolt School' was attended by twenty-five pupils whereas the National School had only five pupils on its register. Eventually, the government was forced to concede defeat and acknowledge the success of the 'Revolt School'. Soon afterwards, the council was given permission to build a new school at Llandecwyn.

The wider political debate continued and the Welsh Church Act of 1914 led to the disestablishment of the Anglican Church in Wales, finally enacted in 1920.

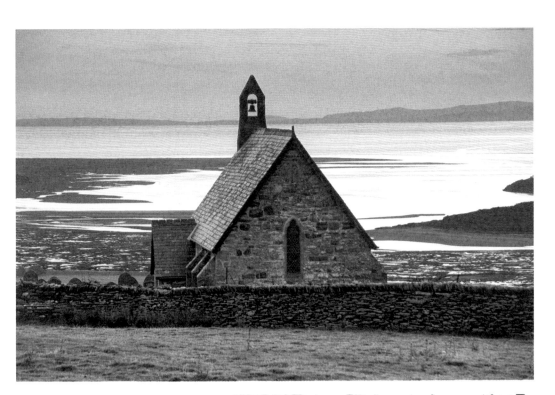

After forking sharply right at Llyn Tecwyn Isaf, the route heads up to Llandecwyn church (*above*), where there's a stunning view of the coastal Morfa and the estuary. The route continues to the upper lake of Llyn Tecwyn Uchaf, where we leave the Ardudwy Way to join the (current) Wales Coast Path. The path follows the left-hand edge of the lake before veering away to enter Coed Felinrhyd forest, turning left on a forest track, as signposted. The path goes straight ahead, where a hairpin bend is joined, and just after the forest road bends right, the path forks left, dropping steeply down a minor track leading to Maentwrog Power Station. The station's twin supply pipeline can be seen across the valley, with its outlet water rushing out into the stream in a torrent (*right*). The path reaches the main road and turns right for a short distance, before turning right on a lane.

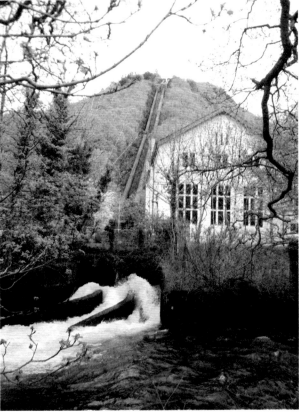

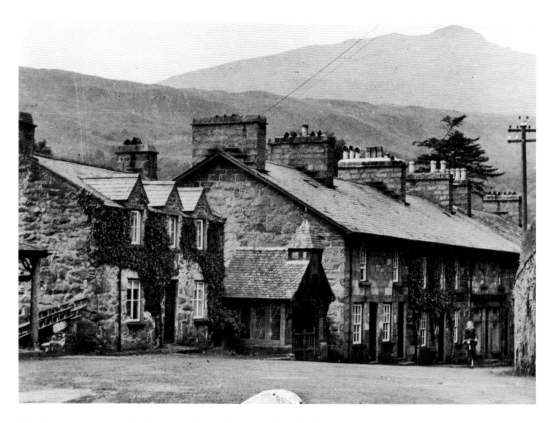

The lane soon passes the huge pipelines that carry the feed water from Trawsfynydd reservoir to the hydroelectric station. The station opened in 1928 with a capacity of 18 megawatts – more than enough to supply the whole of North Wales with electricity at that time. Trawsfynydd reservoir's original dam, built across the Afon Prysor, was the first large arch dam ever built in Britain. The reservoir later served to provide cooling water for Trawsfynydd nuclear power station, which ceased operating in 1991. In the same year, Maentwrog hydro station's capacity was increased to 30 megawatts and it is currently operated by Magnox.

The next section of the route avoids walking along the busy main road and the lane continues uphill for about a mile to Tyn-y-Coed, where it crosses over the pipeline. Just after this, the Coast Path turns left, heading for a ladder stile. From here, the path continues as signposted (signage here has been improved recently). There are great views of the Moelwyns as the path eventually emerges onto a track and turns right to reach a lane. A left turn on the lane leads down past the beautifully restored Old Tannery into Maentwrog village.

The photograph above shows the village street and the lychgate of St Twrog's church in the late nineteenth century. Maentwrog (Twrog's stone) is named after the stone in the churchyard, which, according to legend, was hurled down from the top of the Moelwyns by Twrog, destroying a pagan altar. The stone stands to the east of the south porch (adjacent to the oldest gravestone, dated 1691).

The village expanded in the nineteenth century to house workers from local slate mines and the village inn is called The Grapes, said to be a seventeenth-century coaching inn.

Chapter Two
Maentwrog to Tremadog
10.4 miles (16.7 km)

Between two estuaries to a magical place

This section continues along the Wales Coast Path for most of its route and is reasonably level with few hills. It's a fairly easy day's walk and the path signage through the woodland section has recently been improved.

From Maentwrog village, our route crosses the Afon Dwyryd to Tan-y-Bwlch and passes the Oakeley Arms Hotel. The path then briefly follows the access road towards Plas Tan-y-Bwlch mansion before turning off to pass some waterfalls and reach the attractive lake of Llyn Mair. We cross the Ffestiniog Railway line and keep the famous narrow-gauge railway company for much of our route through woodland towards Penrhyndeudraeth. The route then passes through Pen-y-Bwlch and Penrhyndeudraeth village and follows the main road for about a mile before turning left just after Minffordd station to zig-zag across the Portmeirion peninsula. An opportunity to visit the magical village of Portmeirion should definitely not be missed! The route then crosses over 'The Cob' embankment on the combined cycle path and footway. The embankment is shared with the road and the Ffestiniog Railway and leads us into Porthmadog, with its railway terminus and harbour.

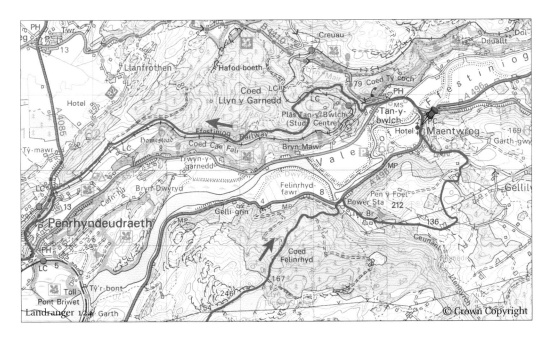

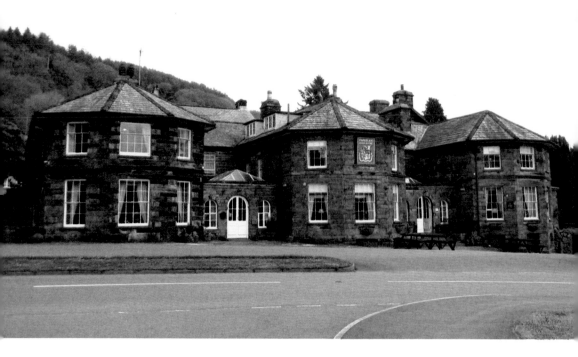

The route leaves the Coast Path at Porthmadog to follow along the impressive High Street, passing the Royal Sportsman Hotel, before turning left alongside 'Y Cyt' (a small canal) on a track which leads under the bypass road to finally reach Tremadog and its market square.

Starting from Maentwrog, the path goes over the old river bridge and crosses the busy main road to reach the Oakeley Arms Hotel (*above*). The hotel was originally known as the Tan-y-Bwlch Inn and the present building dates from the eighteenth century. In its time it has served as a makeshift courthouse and police station and was renamed in the 1840s. It was auctioned off from the estate it served in 1910 and its fortunes have ebbed and flowed since. By the turn of the present century, the building was in a sad state of decay but the present owners have dedicated themselves to restoring the hotel to its former glory.

The path continues along the entrance road to Plas Tan-y-Bwlch, once the residence of the wealthy Oakeley family, owners of the huge slate quarry at Blaenau Ffestiniog. The mansion is now the home of the Snowdonia National Park Environmental Studies Centre and the gardens are open to the public through the year.

About 200 metres before the big house, the path turns sharply right off the access road to follow a pleasant woodland track past some pretty waterfalls up to Llyn Mair lake. The path follows the left shore briefly before forking left up a waymarked track, continuing straight ahead at a timber barrier before forking left as directed. The Ffestiniog Railway line is crossed (stop, look and listen!) and the path reaches a T-junction in a forest clearance area, where a left turn is taken. The signs are then followed as we eventually pass over the dam of a little reservoir and turn left, continuing as the railway reappears down to our left. The path veers away, up through the woods and down again, over a wall, meandering on to reach the high wall of the railway embankment. After crossing a footbridge over a stream, the path goes left and rejoins the railway, turning right alongside the railway wall. The Coast Path signs are then followed past the signal box and Rhiw Goch and along a lane to reach the main road into Penrhyndeudraeth.

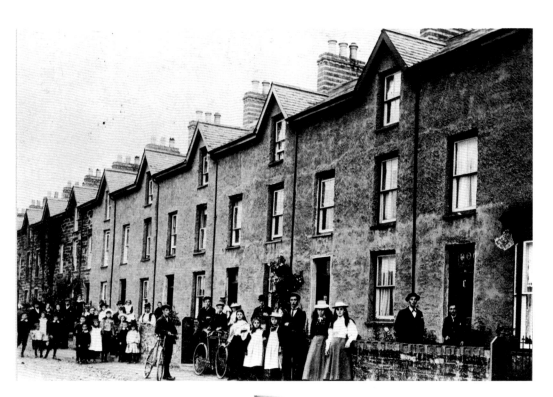

A sharp left turn leads down to a tunnel under the railway and we follow the signs through Pen-y-Bwlch to eventually turn left into the centre of Penrhyndeudraeth. The village's name can be translated into 'headland between two beaches', describing its situation between Traeth Mawr, which is the Glaslyn estuary (now largely reclaimed), and Traeth Bach, which is the Dwyryd estuary. The village centre is at a crossroads where our route turns right to follow the main road for about a mile towards Minffordd. After about 300 metres, just past a chapel, there's a row of houses on the left called Heol Eryri (Eryri Terrace) and the charming photograph above shows some of its residents in their Sunday best around 1915.

The route soon passes Minffordd Station and the picture to the right shows the Ffestiniog Railway's *Merddin Emrys* leaving the station. This Double Fairlie loco was built in 1879.

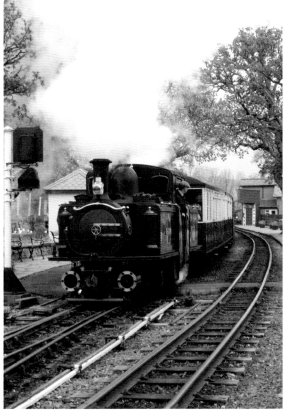

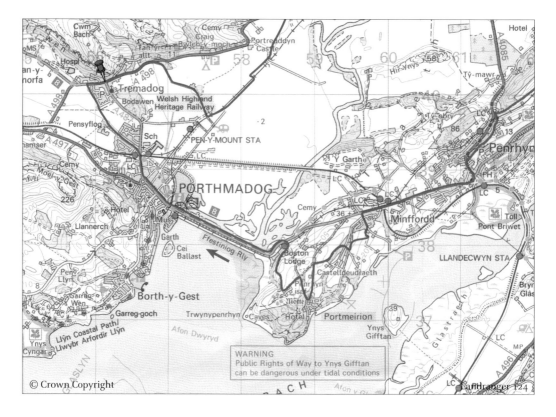

The Coast Path turns left and passes the Portmeirion access road, continuing along the lane until, just after the end of the houses, it turns right through a gate onto a track. It then turns right along a field edge to the top corner where it turns left on a bridleway, turning right at a cottage and crossing the access road before continuing on a track, which bends around left. Passing through a gate, the path follows the field edge to a large barn, where it turns left on another bridleway. The path continues down to a gate at the bottom, where the car park and entrance to Portmeirion are to the left.

The unique village of Portmeirion was created by the celebrated architect and conservationist Sir Clough Williams-Ellis, who acquired the site in 1925 and spent the next fifty years of his life transforming this naturally beautiful, but neglected, peninsula into a magical place. With its fascinating buildings and magnificent gardens, Portmeirion now attracts around 240,000 visitors a year.

Historically, there was once a medieval castle on the peninsula and later a little port called Aber lâ, which, by the 1850s, became the location of a 'beautiful mansion' called Aberia. Clough changed the name to Portmeirion, opening it as a hotel, and set about creating a village with incredibly imaginative buildings using a wide range of architectural styles. His genius for salvaging structures and fittings from demolition sites and incorporating them into his designs has created what he described as 'a home for fallen buildings'. His motto was 'Cherish the Past; Adorn the Present; Construct for the Future'. Although Portmeirion is famous for the filming of *The Prisoner* (starring Patrick McGoohan), Clough thought that Portmeirion stole the show from its human cast!

Portmeirion's appealing cottages have names such as Dolphin, Mermaid, Angel, Unicorn, Anchor and Fountain and provide unique accommodation options to complement the famous hotel.

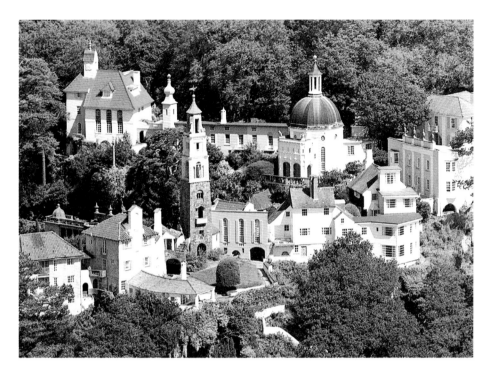

Prominent in the aerial view of Portmeirion above is the Bell Tower built by Clough in 1928 as an early dramatic gesture and 'embodying stones from the twelfth-century castle of his ancestor'. The domed Pantheon of 1960 remedied the village's 'dome deficiency'!

The quayside at dawn (*below*) features the Portmeirion Hotel and the *Amis Reunis*, which is neither ship nor building. When Portmeirion opened, Clough bought and converted a 70-ton ketch, which he moored alongside the quay. During a sudden gale, she was carried to the island and wrecked and Clough resolved to reconstruct her as a 'ship aground'.

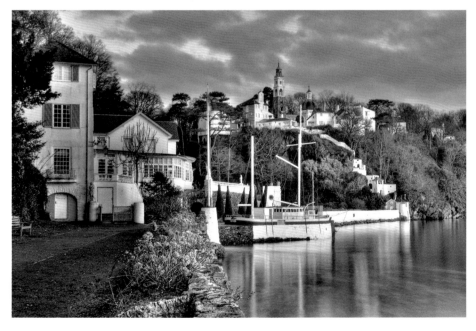

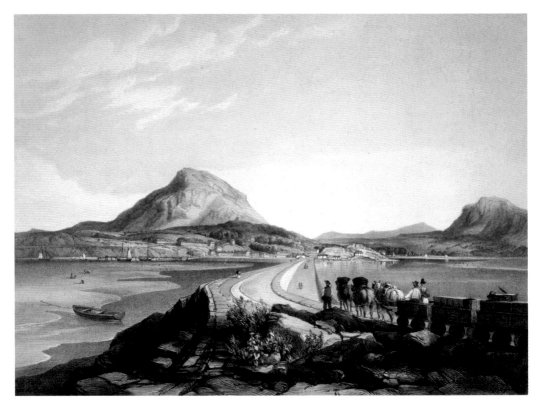

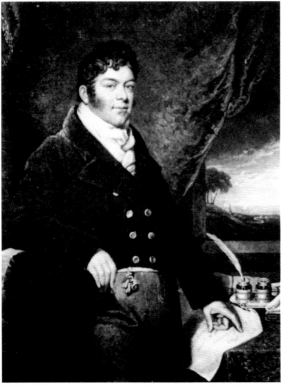

From Portmeirion, the Coast Path turns sharply back on itself, passing up through a couple of gates to a crossroads in the tracks, where it turns left on a bridleway. Passing Penrhyn Isaf, it heads towards a gate on the other side of the field. We don't go through this gate, but turn right along the field edge then cross the field to another gate in the distance. The next section leads down through trees towards Boston Lodge, with a great view of the Cob causeway to the left. It's a magical view, with Porthmadog in the distance and the hill of Moel-y-Gest behind, and its history is captured in the nineteenth-century painting above. The Cob embankment was built by William Madocks (*left*) between 1807 and 1811 to reclaim agricultural land from the Glaslyn estuary and to create a new harbour at Porthmadog, the port that bears his name.

To reach the Cob, the Coast Path crosses the Ffestiniog Railway track near Boston Lodge Halt and drops down to the busy main road. We cross over carefully to the footway on the other side, turning left and joining the cycle route over the embankment (this should not be used during periods of flooding). The route soon passes the old toll house on our left. Tolls ended in 2003 but the tariff board on the toll house reminds us of a bygone age.

The Cob embankment was one of the engineering feats of the age and opened in 1811 to huge acclaim and much celebration. Unfortunately, a great storm shortly afterwards caused severe damage and repairs took another three years to complete. In the 1830s, the Ffestiniog Railway was constructed on the causeway, with the toll road on the inland side. The Cob withstood many violent storms over the years and in 2001 was strengthened with a wider roadway and a footway/cycleway on a new embankment.

The popular Ffestiniog Railway runs for 13½ miles from Blaenau Ffestiniog to Porthmadog and was originally built to carry slate from the quarries to Porthmadog Harbour. Hitherto, slate had been hauled by pack horse to the River Dwyryd, from where it was conveyed by boat. In the railway's early days, the slate wagons were operated by gravity and horsepower until steam locomotives were introduced in 1863. The following year, passenger services began and as slate traffic increased, the more powerful Double Fairlie locomotives were introduced. By the 1920s, however, slate traffic on the line was declining and shortly after the Second World War, the line was closed and abandoned. From 1951 onwards, the line was gradually restored and, thanks to the efforts of many dedicated people, it finally reached Blaenau Ffestiniog in 1982, almost 150 years to the day after it was started.

The photograph below shows Porthmadog Harbour Station in 1906, with sailing ships in the port.

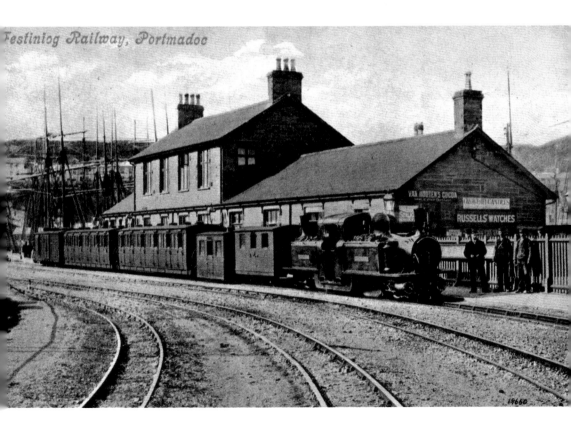

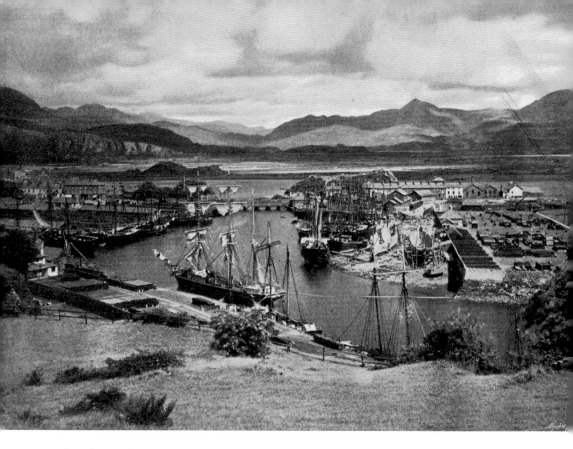

Porthmadog Harbour Station is the terminus of the Ffestiniog and Welsh Highland Railways and has Spooner's Café & Bar handily situated on the platform. After we cross the Pont Britannia bridge, a left turn takes us to the harbour, which once bustled with shipbuilding and the loading of slate onto sailing vessels for export around the world. It's pleasant to explore the harbour, and a walk past the harbourmaster's office and a climb up the Grisiau Mawr (Big Steps) towards the Garth is rewarded with a great view of the harbour and the mountains. The slate was brought here on the Ffestiniog Railway and also by smaller boats from wharves along the Afon Dwyryd. The photograph above shows the harbour in the late nineteenth century with its shipyards and slate wharves and, in the foreground, a fine three-masted sailing barque is moored alongside, ready for loading.

 The port's heyday was probably around the 1870s, when over a thousand ships a year used the harbour. In 1873, no less than 116,000 tons of slate was exported from Porthmadog but, by the 1880s, export of slate and the local shipping industry were declining. The port's commercial activities were effectively ended by the outbreak of the First World War. The arrival of the Cambrian main line railway in 1867 contributed to the downturn but also brought tourists to the area. Porthmadog's ideal location for exploring the beauties of Snowdonia continues to attract many visitors.

 It's difficult to appreciate that the town of Porthmadog, with its splendid main street, was once marshland that flooded at high tide. The foresight of William Madocks enabled this whole area to be reclaimed, and the town rightly carries his name (Porthmadog translates to 'Madog's Port'). There's another theory, however, that suggests the name derives from the legend of Prince Madog, who reputedly discovered America in the twelfth century!

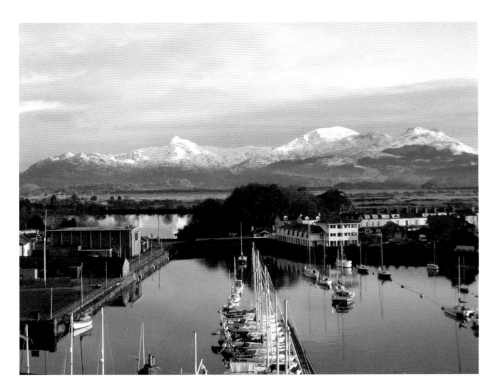

Porthmadog Harbour is now the home of leisure yachts and the stunning view from the Garth (*above*) looks out over the moorings with the Llyn Bach flood control pool on the other side of the bridge. The snow-capped mountains include Cnicht and the Moelwyns.

Our route leaves the Coast Path behind to follow along Porthmadog's High Street, pictured below in the early 1900s. The old town hall, with its clock tower, was later demolished. The High Street bends right and continues past the celebrated Royal Sportsman Hotel.

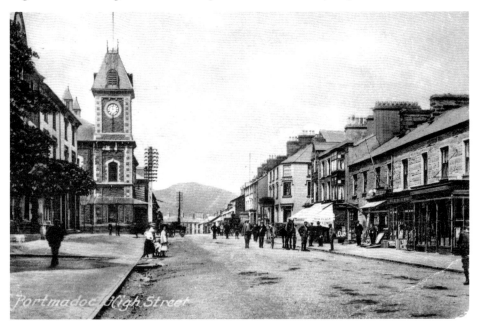

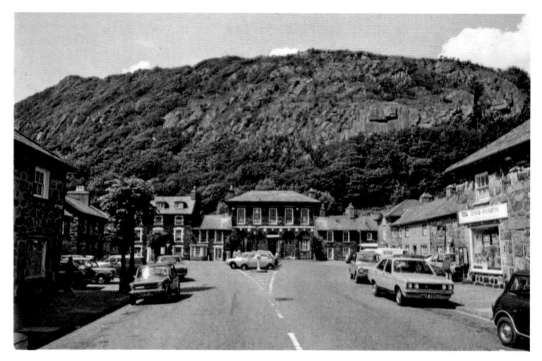

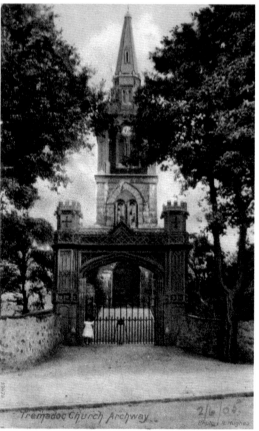

After crossing the main railway line, the route turns left and follows 'Y Cut', a little canal built for Madocks to drain the Traeth. Forking right, the footpath follows the Cut for a bit further before crossing over it and continuing through a bridge under the bypass road. The path reaches the main A498 road, where we turn right into the village of Tremadog and its attractive Market Square, pictured above in the 1970s.

Tremadog was laid out as a 'model village' on marshland reclaimed by Madocks, and its centre was completed by 1811. The imposing central square, with its stylish buildings and several welcoming inns, has the sheer cliff as a backdrop. On the road leading out of the square is the early nineteenth-century Gothic Revival church, with its archway entrance charmingly portrayed (*left*). The church has been tastefully converted into a community centre while the village chapel, almost opposite, has a neo-classical façade and provides the religious balance much favoured by Madocks.

Chapter Three

Tremadog to Pen-y-Gwryd
16.6 miles (26.7 km)

The Pass of Aberglaslyn and the legend of Gelert

This long section passes through some of the loveliest scenery in Snowdonia and may be conveniently split at Beddgelert if a two-day walk is preferred. The route climbs very gradually for the 900-foot ascent to Pen-y-Gwryd and there are few steep climbs. The short section across fields near Pont Croesor can become waterlogged and gaiters and spare socks (or even wellingtons!) are recommended here. The path through the Aberglaslyn Pass is rocky and slippery and care is needed. The route passes Gelert's grave and the attractive village of Beddgelert before visiting the beautiful lakes of Llyn Dinas and Llyn Gwynant, finally reaching the Pen-y-Gwryd Hotel, famous for its mountaineering connections.

Leaving Tremadog, our route goes along High Street, passing Tan yr Allt on our left side with a good view of the old corn mill, sadly now derelict. Tan yr Allt was the home of William Madocks, Tremadog's founder and, interestingly, the poet Shelley lived here around 1813. He apparently made a hasty departure after an alleged attempt on his life by a nocturnal intruder!

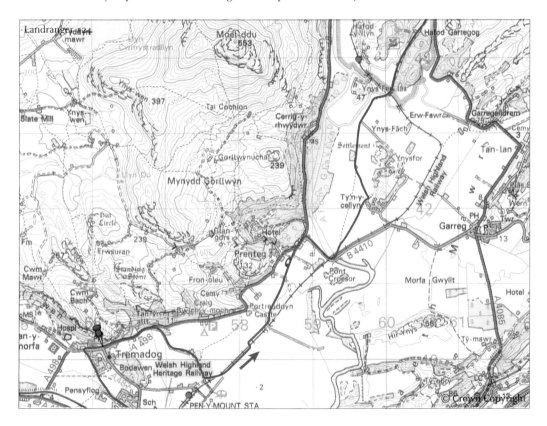

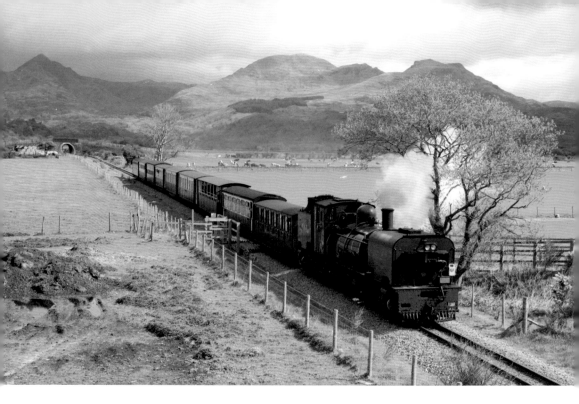

We follow the right-hand side of the A498 road for about 0.4 miles, firstly on footway, then keeping carefully to the grass verge for about 400 yards before forking right on a bridleway. The bridleway leads down through Farmyard to reach the Welsh Highland Railway line at Cynfal, where we carefully cross the track and turn left on a footpath alongside the railway. The line is crossed again just after passing a bridge and the path continues along the field edge towards another bridge with a great view of Cnicht and the Moelwyns ahead. The Welsh Highland Railway (*above*) has restored a long-lost link between Porthmadog and Caernarfon and runs for 25 miles through the magnificent scenery of the National Park. It uses the largest 2-foot-gauge steam locomotives in the world.

We bear left onto a track just before the bridge, then right over a ladder stile, turning left on a path that leads on to the main road at Prenteg. Continuing along the verge, we turn right on the B4410 road towards Pont Croesor. This straight quarter-mile section has no verge or footpath, so care is needed. At Pont Croesor, there's a public viewing point, where the nesting site of the Glaslyn ospreys may be observed. Our ongoing route passes the nesting site and great care must be taken not to disturb the birds.

We cross the railway just after Pont Croesor bridge and the footpath angles across to a ladder stile. The fields are very boggy here and can become waterlogged, so gaiters and spare socks (or even wellingtons!) are recommended. This is the most direct route towards Aberglaslyn – the alternatives are a long way around. The footpath crosses a ditch and continues straight towards Ty'n-y-cellyn farm, heading for the left side of the barn. There are two posts sticking up, indicating a little bridge across the ditch – it's very boggy again here where the cattle have been. We cross over a stone stile to the left of the barn, veering right through a gate, then immediately left to follow the right-hand side (not the left side) of the hedge line to reach an embankment.

We follow the embankment around, walking quietly and keeping moving so as not to disturb the birds. The embankment eventually leads to a little metal footbridge down on the left, leading to another railway crossing and a lane. The lane passes Hafod Garregog up to the A4085 road, crossing and continuing straight ahead to Bwlchgwernog. A left turn is taken here, by a low white cottage, along a lane that leads to the attractive village of Nantmor. We pass the chapel and Hen Ysgol (the old school) before crossing the railway again near Nantmor station. At the main road we turn right to reach Aberglaslyn National Trust car park on our right. At the top left-hand corner of the car park, there's a gate and sign pointing left to Aberglaslyn, up some steps. The path leads around and descends some very steep, rocky steps to Pont Aberglaslyn – a popular beauty spot since Victorian times as shown in the photograph below, taken around 1860.

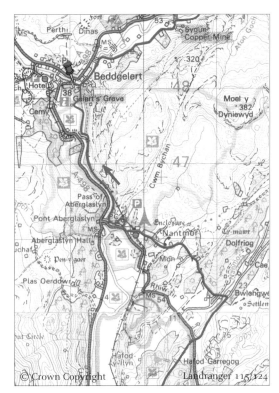

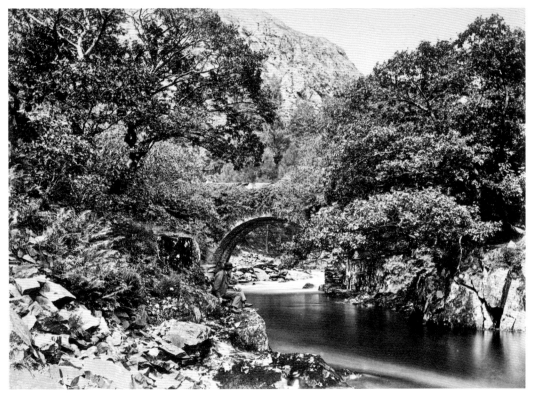

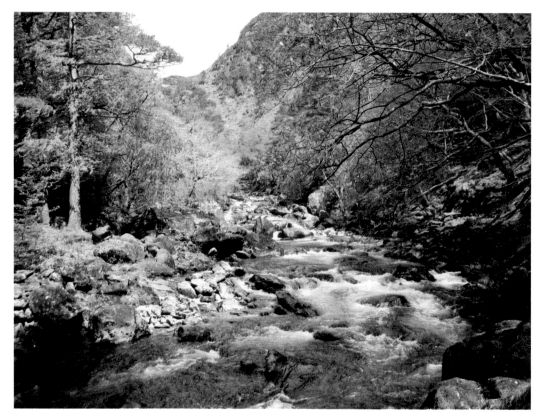

We continue along the right-hand side of the river, proceeding with great care as the path is close to the rushing torrent and is very rocky and slippery. There's a section next to the water's edge where there are iron rings in the rock, providing handholds.

This is the scenic Pass of Aberglaslyn, with its lovely cascades and rapids (*above*), and has been visited by many travellers, including George Borrow in 1854. The scene soon opens out and the view towards Beddgelert was, to Borrow's eyes, 'very grand and beautiful'.

The path becomes more level as it moves slightly away from the river with the Welsh Highland Railway to the right. We cross the railway line and then a footbridge over the river to continue along its left side. We pass through a fancy carved gate then, immediately after another gate, turn left to visit Gelert's grave (*left*).

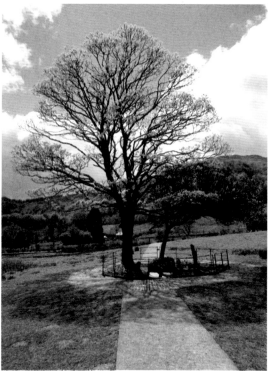

The legend of Gelert the dog is related on a tablet at the graveside and tells the story of the faithful hound who was left behind by his master, Prince Llywelyn, when he went on a hunting trip. The dog was left to guard the cot of Llywelyn's baby son, but when his master returned and Gelert leapt to greet him, the dog had blood around his mouth and the baby was nowhere to be seen. In his anger, Llywelyn drew his sword and killed the dog only to find, nearby, the body of a great wolf that had been killed by Gelert. The baby was still safe under his overturned cot and had been protected from the wolf by the dog. The remorseful Llywelyn buried the dog with honour at this spot and it is said that, from that day onward, Llywelyn never smiled again. When George Borrow visited the spot he found the legend to be 'singularly beautiful and affecting' and observed that no one could visit the grave without exclaiming with a sigh, 'Poor Gelert!'

We continue on the path through a gap in the wall, then turn right back towards the river, where we turn left and continue alongside the Afon Glaslyn to its confluence with the Afon Colwyn. Up to our left, Beddgelert's very own mountain, Moel Hebog, looks proudly down on the village. A left turn by the footbridge takes us into the centre of the village and the old stone bridge.

Beddgelert is translated as 'Gelert's Grave' and the village is popularly said to derive its name from the legend of the dog Gelert. A more prosaic alternative is the grave of Celert, an early Christian saint. The attractive print by Hugh Hughes below depicts Beddgelert Bridge in 1845, with Moel Hebog mountain overlooking the village.

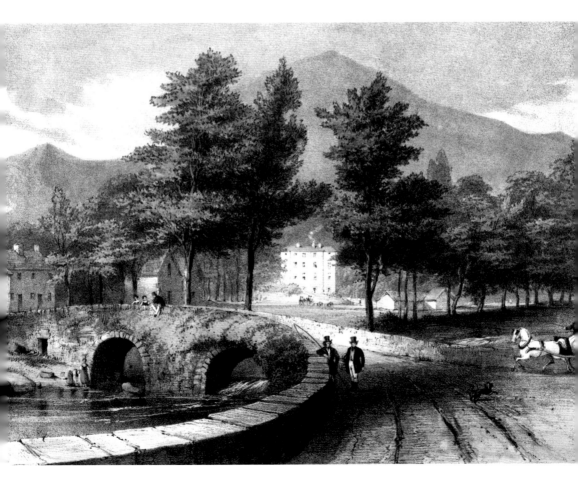

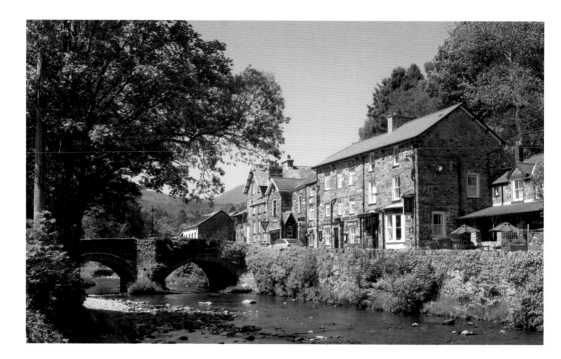

The Prince Llewelyn Hotel on the right-hand side of the bridge (*above*) is a friendly and welcoming place, unlike the hotel Borrow stayed at in 'Beth Gelert' in 1854, where he described the company as 'disagreeable enough'!

We leave Beddgelert by crossing the footbridge near the confluence of the rivers and continue along the right-hand side of the Afon Glaslyn. We follow the lane past the entrance to Sygun Fawr country house hotel to reach the old Sygun Copper Mine.

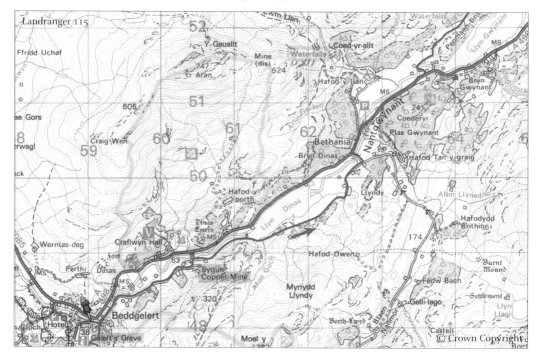

Sygun Copper Mine is open to the public, mainly between March and November, and offers an opportunity to explore old workings, tunnels and colourful chambers with stalactite and stalagmite formations. Sygun's hillside consists of some of the oldest rocks in Wales, created by volcanic activity some 450 million years ago. The rock contains deposits of different minerals, mainly copper ore, but traces of precious metals have also been found. The ore mined here was crushed and the copper ore was separated from the waste rock on a 'jigging' table – a sieve with water running through, causing the copper ore to sink to the bottom. The crushing and jigging machinery were powered by waterwheels supplied by a leat from nearby Llyn Dinas. The mine's busiest period was the first half of the nineteenth century but it closed in 1903. It reopened as a visitor attraction in 1986 after much restoration.

At the Copper Mine we turn left to join the 'Lakeside Walk', which goes right, before the bridge, initially along the right-hand side of the river and with a great view of the Nantgwynant Valley ahead. On reaching the peaceful and beautiful Llyn Dinas (*below*), the path follows around the right-hand side of the lake. The path soon edges away from the lake, up the bank, and enters the woods before dropping down again and continuing across a marshy area. The path crosses a couple of ladder stiles then continues as waymarked to eventually pass through the yard of Llyndy Isaf. The route continues along the farm track to the entrance gate, turning left to cross over the Glaslyn and reach the main road, which we cross carefully to a parking area on the other side. This is Bethania and just along to the right is the old chapel, tastefully converted into the Caffi Gwynant, very popular with walkers and an ideal refreshment stop. This is the starting point of the Watkin Path route up Snowdon.

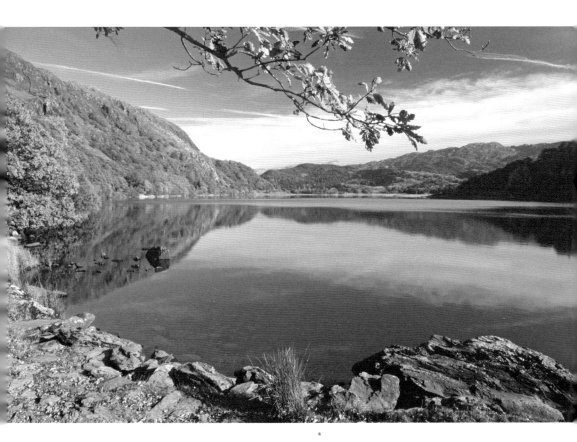

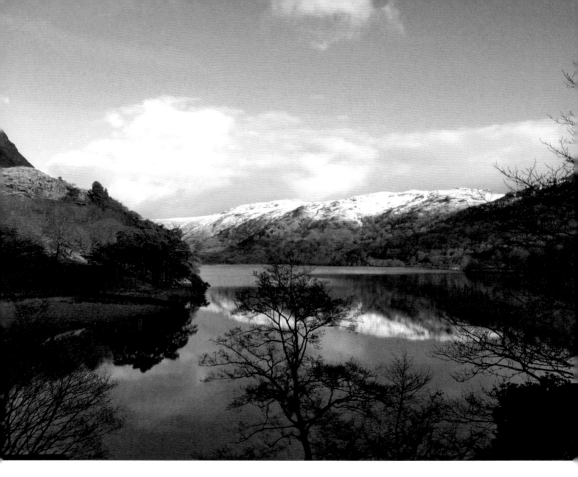

Our route follows the footway along the left side of the road, past the start of the Watkin Path, continuing along a short section of narrow verge before it becomes footway again. After about three quarters of a mile, just past the entrance to Pen y Bryn Isaf, we turn left at a footpath sign, through a gate and down to a ladder stile. We continue to another gate and cross a charming little footbridge over the infant Glaslyn river. The path bends right to join the track, which winds around towards a farmhouse. After a small ruined building we turn left on a path, just before the farmhouse, turning left to follow a wall for a short distance to reach another track, on which we turn right through a gap in the wall. The stony track continues ahead, joining another wall for a short distance before Llyn Gwynant lake (*above*) comes into view.

The path reaches a gate and ladder stile before continuing through trees and climbing steeply above the lake. Great care is needed along a tricky section, with steep drops down to the right. This leads to a magnificent viewpoint above Elephant Rock, so called due to its shape when viewed from the other side of the lake. The path continues on a steep bank with views of the lake through the trees, and reaches a ladder stile over a wall at the top of the lake. The lithograph opposite shows a view of Llyn Gwynant from the north-east, with Elephant Rock on the right side of the lake.

The stony path continues, following the left side of the river and meandering very pleasantly between the rocks and the trees. The path passes very close to the fast-flowing stream before continuing across a marshy area and over a ladder stile to reach Cwm Dyli Power Station.

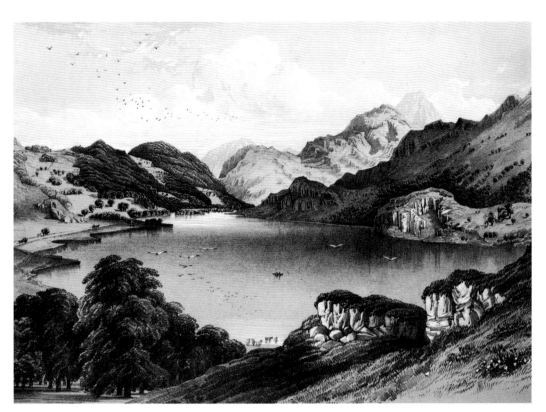

The hydroelectric station is fed by a 2-kilometre-long pipeline from Llyn Llydaw, high up on the flanks of Snowdon. The station was commissioned in 1906 to provide power for the local slate and mining industry and also powered the transatlantic transmitting station set up by Marconi in 1914, near the village of Waunfawr. It currently supplies 9.9 megawatts of green energy to the grid and is one of the oldest grid-connected hydroelectric stations in the world.

We cross over the pipeline and follow the track around to the main gate, following the access road around to the right to join the track going up the valley. We turn sharply left here and, although there's a gradual climb on this last section, the views of Snowdon up to the left and the valley behind offer great compensation. We come out alongside the main road, following the left side up to the Pen-y-Gwryd Hotel.

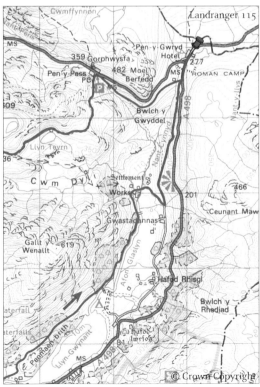

33

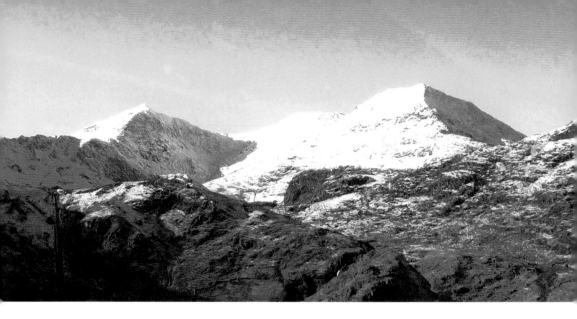

Snowdon is pictured above in winter, but our ascent is planned for milder conditions! The Pen-y-Gwryd Hotel is the perfect place to stay before and after the climb and has impeccable mountaineering connections. It was a training base for the first successful ascent of Mount Everest in June 1953 and the photograph below was taken at a reunion of the Everest party on 18 October 1953. It shows (not in order) Wilfred Noyce, George Lowe, Tom Stobart, Sir Edmund Hillary, Emlyn Jones, Charles Evans, Alfred Gregory, Sir John Hunt, Tom Bourdillon, Mike Westmacott, Charles Wylie, Anthony Rawlinson, George Band and Michael Ward.

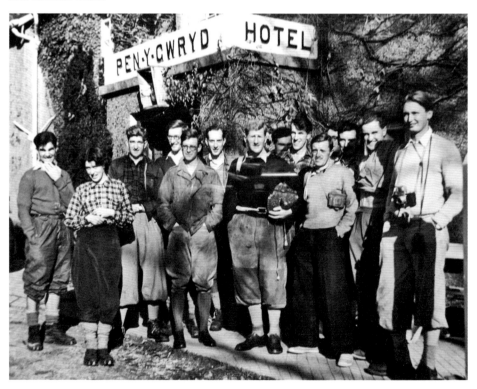

Chapter Four

Pen-y-Gwryd to Llanberis

10.0 miles (16.1 km)

The Ascent of Yr Wyddfa

Today we walk up to Pen-y-Pass and climb Snowdon by the Miners' Track, descending on the Llanberis Path. The climb is a steep and strenuous rocky route, including scree, with an ascent of over 2,700 feet and a descent of nearly 3,300 feet. It's recommended that the climb is carried out in good, clear summer weather when the walk is safer and the views are spectacular – conditions in wintertime can be very severe indeed. It's important that a weather forecast is obtained in advance as weather conditions can change very rapidly. Proper mountain equipment must be used, including warm, waterproof clothing and proper footwear as well as a map, compass and whistle and adequate rations.

Before leaving, an exploration of the Pen-y-Gwryd Hotel is a must. Particularly interesting is the room with signatures on the ceiling of great climbers, including the teams that achieved the first ascent of Everest in 1953 and first ascent of Kangchenjunga in 1955. With its climbing memorabilia and unique atmosphere, the hotel can truly be described as a 'home for British mountaineering'.

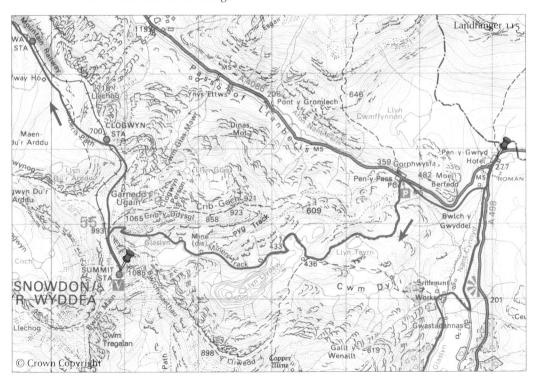

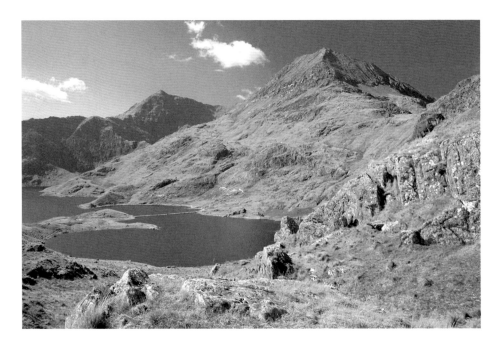

The route from the hotel returns past the road junction down to where the old track joins on the right. A signpost here points to Pen-y-Pass along a footpath that follows a route below the road and up to Pen-y-Pass. The main road should be avoided.

From Pen-y-Pass car park we follow the Miners' Track, signposted on a gate in the far left corner. It's very important to keep to the designated track all the way to the summit. The Miner's Track was originally constructed to serve the Britannia Copper Mine and winds around the side of the hill, passing Llyn Teyrn to our left, where there are ruins of old miners' barracks. There's a great sense of anticipation as we proceed upwards. The photograph above of Snowdon and Crib Goch was taken from The Horns, up above the Miners' Track.

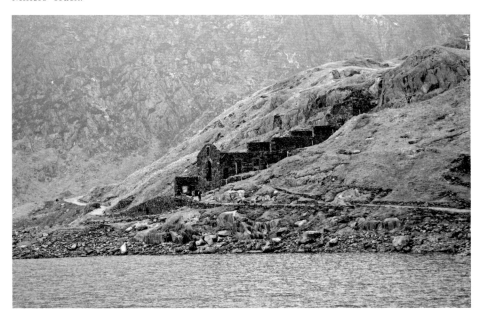

We pass the pipeline that feeds Cwm Dyli Power Station on our left before forking right to reach the causeway across Llyn Llydaw. The causeway was built in 1853 to enable horse-drawn copper wagons to cross the lake. The wagons and horses were previously floated across Llyn Llydaw on rafts, until an accident occurred in which a horse was drowned. Crossing the causeway we follow the lake around left to reach the remains of the Britannia Copper Mine crushing mill (*opposite below*). Copper mining on Snowdon was taking place from around 1800 and various mining companies were active before the mine closed in 1916.

After the old workings, the Miners' Track edges away from the lake, climbing more steeply to reach the glacial lake of Glaslyn. We follow around the right side of Glaslyn and, just after some ruined barracks, we turn right and really start to climb, following the steep track up the scree. This part of the track is a hard climb and can be very slippery – it is best avoided in winter conditions. The Miners' Track eventually joins the Pyg Track coming up from the right and we turn left on the combined path. It's said that the Pyg Track is named after the initial letters of the Pen-y-Gwryd (Hotel).

The track continues to climb steeply and loose underfoot and we approach the Zig-Zags, keeping well away from open mine shafts on the left. The Zig-Zags climb up to the standing stone on the ridge at Bwlch Glas and we turn left, joining the Llanberis path towards the summit with the Snowdon Mountain Railway track to our right. A final push takes us up to the Trig Point on the summit of Snowdon (Yr Wyddfa) at 3,560 feet (1,085 metres), the highest peak in Wales. The views on a clear day are sensational and the panorama below shows Llyn Llydaw and the knife-edge ridge of Crib Goch.

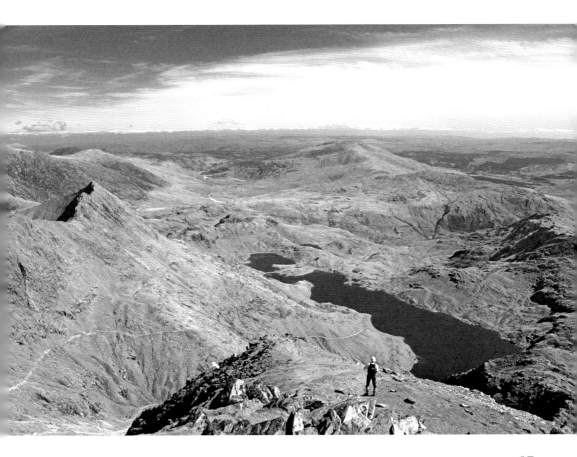

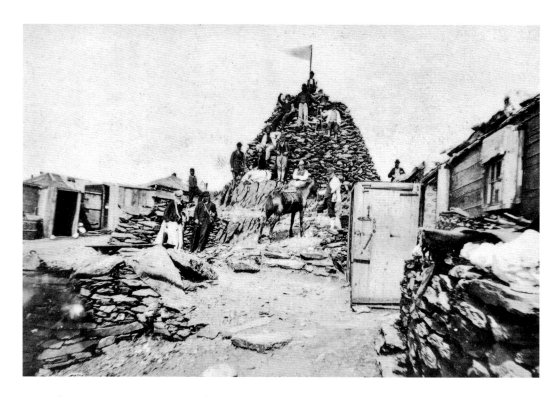

The scene greeting us at Snowdon's summit has changed greatly since the photograph above of 'hotels' on the summit was taken in the 1870s. There have been various buildings here since the 1830s, and a liquor licence was first obtained in 1845. A station building designed by Sir Clough Williams-Ellis was erected in the 1930s to replace the previous dilapidated structures and this was demolished to make way for Hafod Eryri, the award-winning visitor centre (*below*), which was officially opened by the Rt Hon Rhodri Morgan AM, First Minister of Wales, on 12 June 2009.

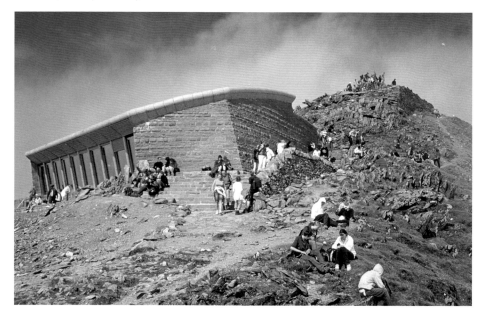

George Borrow climbed Yr Wyddfa from Llanberis in 1854, accompanied by his daughter, Henrietta, and a guide. At the top, he found 'a rude cabin in which refreshments were sold, and in which a person resided through the year'. He was no doubt delighted to have reached the highest pub in Wales and 'went into the cabin, where Henrietta had some excellent coffee, and himself and the guide a bottle of tolerable ale'. Today's visitor centre was named Hafod Eryri ('summer dwelling in Snowdonia') after a competition to find a name and is a vast improvement on the 'rude cabin' of Borrow's time.

Snowdon's Welsh name, Yr Wyddfa, may be translated as 'the tumulus' and is the legendary burial place of Rhita Gawr, a great giant killed by King Arthur. Rhita Gawr is reputed to have worn a cloak made from the beards of kings he had slain! The mountain has long been associated with Arthurian legend and it's said that the spirits of Merlin and Arthur are still present as well as the Tylwyth Teg fairies.

We start our walk down alongside the Snowdon Mountain Railway track and follow the Llanberis Path, the longest and most gradual of the routes up Snowdon, which mainly follows the railway down. A little further down from the Bwlch Glas standing stone, we keep left, avoiding the path to the right, which leads to the knife-edge ridge of Crib Goch. We rejoin the railway just before Clogwyn Station, going through a bridge under the track. The railway runs for 4.7 miles from Llanberis to the summit and was opened in 1896; before the railway was built, well-heeled visitors employed guides and were carried up Snowdon by mule. The photograph below shows the railway and three trains, including one stopped at Clogwyn Station. The Llanberis Path can be seen passing under the railway bridge and in the distance is Llanberis and Llyn Padarn lake.

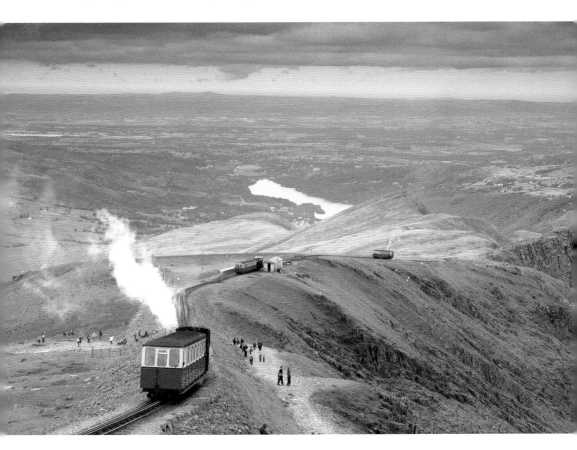

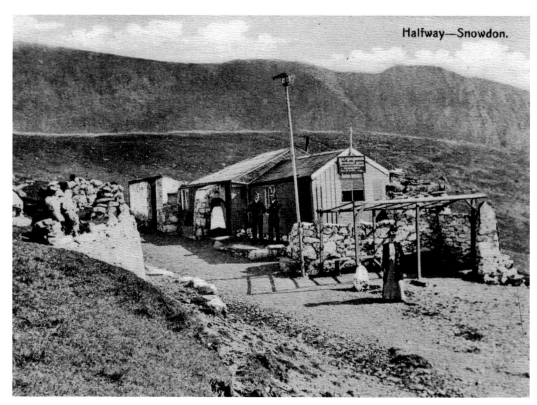

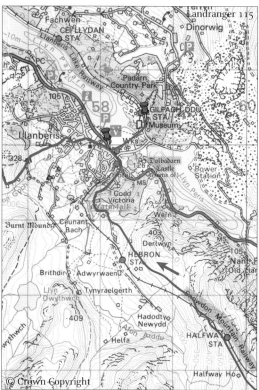

The trains operate from March to November (weather permitting) and the single carriages are pushed up Snowdon by both diesel and steam locomotives. The Snowdon Mountain Railway is the only public rack-and-pinion railway in the British Isles.

Descending with great views of Cwm Brwynog to the left, we reach the Halfway House, pictured above in the early 1900s, where refreshments are still served in the summer months. Continuing down we pass Halfway Station to cross under the railway again, and further on we can see Hebron Station down to the left. The path emerges onto a lane, where we turn right to follow the lane around and down towards Llanberis, passing the Penceunant Tea Rooms. We can see the vast galleries of the old Dinorwig slate quarries looming ahead. The lane emerges at Victoria Terrace, which reaches the main road opposite the Royal Victoria Hotel. A left turn here takes us to the centre of Llanberis.

40

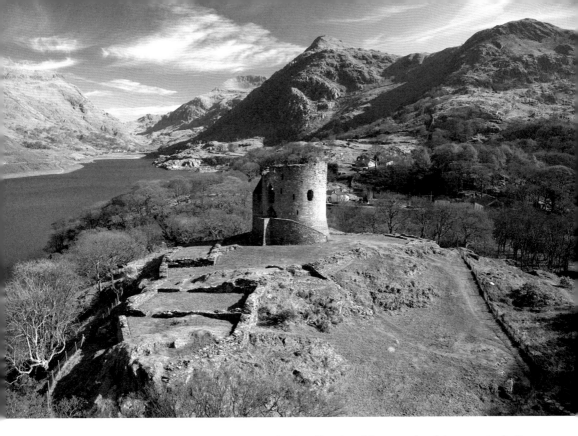

Llanberis is affectionately known as 'Snowdon's Village' and has much of interest, including the National Slate Museum, Electric Mountain Power Station and Padarn Country Park. Firstly, however, we visit the ruins of Dolbadarn Castle by turning right off the main road. The castle remains are on the bank up to the right and the tower stands proudly guarding the Pass of Llanberis, between the twin lakes of Llyn Peris and Llyn Padarn.

The castle was built by the mighty Welsh Prince Llywelyn Fawr (Llywelyn the Great) sometime before 1230 and it was active during the struggles for control of North Wales in the thirteenth century. His grandson, Llywelyn ap Gruffydd, Prince of Wales, imprisoned his older brother Owain Goch here for twenty years and, during the revolt against the English monarch Edward I, Dolbadarn was held by Llywelyn's other brother, Dafydd. Prince Llywelyn was ambushed and killed at the hands of the English in 1282 and in the same year, Dolbadarn Castle fell to English forces. Dafydd was later captured and taken to Shrewsbury, accused of treason against the King, and was condemned to death. He was tied to a horse and dragged through the streets of Shrewsbury before being hung, drawn and quartered. He was the first notable person known to have been executed by this gruesome method. To further subdue the Welsh, Edward I built his great ring of castles in North Wales, including those at Harlech, Caernarfon and Beaumaris. The aerial photograph above shows Dolbadarn Castle and Llyn Peris, looking towards Snowdon.

The road passing Dolbadarn Castle leads around to Electric Mountain, an incredible feat of engineering hidden in the Elidir Mountain behind the vast galleries of the old Dinorwig slate quarry. The power station may be visited by guided mini-bus tour from the Electric Mountain Centre in Llanberis.

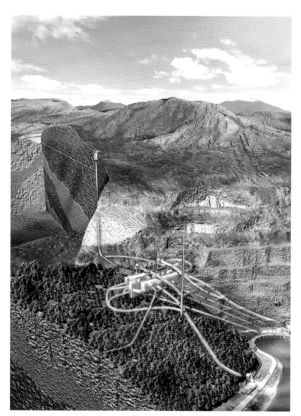

The entrance to the hydroelectric station is alongside Llyn Peris and it's difficult to believe there are miles of tunnels hidden inside the mountain, as shown in the cutaway view (*left*). A gigantic cavern has been carved out of the sheer rock and is said to be the largest underground chamber ever excavated by man. The chamber contains massive inlet valves and fast response turbine generators that go from zero to full power in seconds. The station pumps water from Llyn Peris through huge pipes in the mountain up to the Marchlyn Mawr reservoir during the night, when electricity demand is low. At periods of peak demand, the process is reversed and the water is released back downwards to power the turbines and generate up to 1728 megawatts of electricity for the grid.

This is all a far cry from the slate quarrying days at Dinorwig illustrated below, with large slabs of slate being split on the gallery floor.

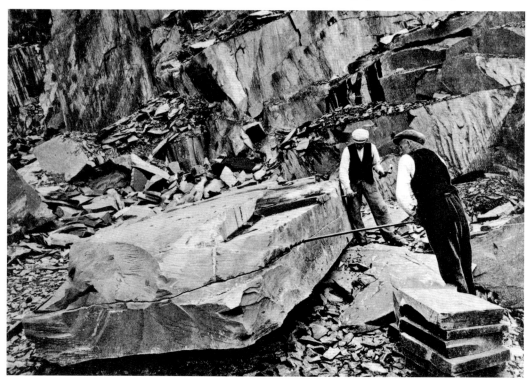

Chapter Five
Llanberis to Caernarfon
10.3 miles (16.5 km)

To where Princes are crowned

Today's walk is fairly easy going, apart from a steady climb of about 850 feet at the start. From Llanberis we follow part of the Snowdonia Marathon route on a narrow lane and track over to Waunfawr. The route ascends to open moorland at Bwlch-y-groes, with great views back towards Llanberis. We pass old slate tips, with views of the Snowdonia mountains, and drop down to the village of Waunfawr with views ahead of Caernarfon and the Menai Strait. From Waunfawr there's a combination of byway and public path leading to Bontnewydd, including part of the Lôn Gwyrfai cycle route. The route from Bontnewydd to Caernarfon follows a section of the Llyn Coastal Path, which shares its route with the Lôn Eifion cycle track alongside the Welsh Highland Railway. The day's walk reaches the magnificent Caernarfon Castle and the chapter ends with an exploration of the Royal Town of Caernarfon.

Before leaving Llanberis, however, there's much to explore, including the National Slate Museum and Padarn Country Park. The best starting point is the Electric Mountain Centre, where there's a souvenir shop, café and tourist office, as well as the booking point for the tours to Electric Mountain. Along the main road from the centre, there's a gate leading to a footpath that passes behind the bus turning area and follows the edge of the sports field alongside the Llanberis Lake Railway towards Gilfach Ddu and the Slate Museum.

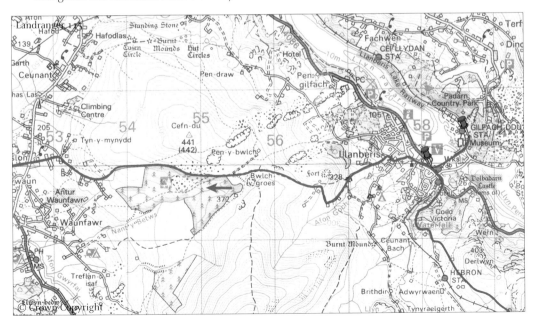

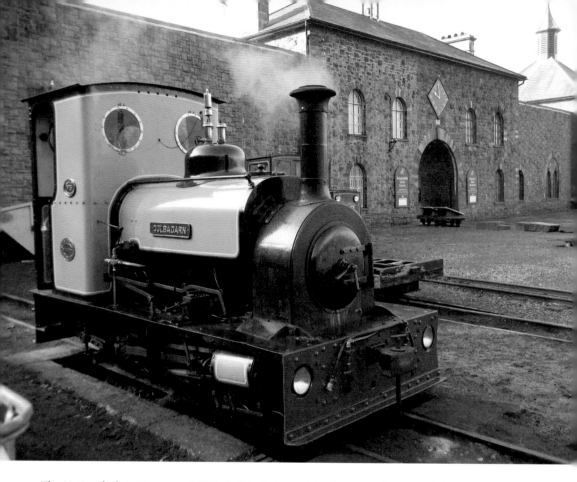

The National Slate Museum at Gilfach Ddu is housed in the magnificent workshop buildings of the Dinorwig Quarry and since it opened in 1972 has attracted over three million visitors. The photograph above shows the locomotive *Dolbadarn* outside the Slate Museum, getting up steam ready for hauling a train on the Llanberis Lake Railway. The narrow-gauge railway follows part of the old slate railway route and uses some the quarry's original locomotives; the *Dolbadarn* was built for Dinorwig Quarry in 1922. The railway runs alongside Llyn Padarn amid the lovely scenery of the Country Park, where there are also many walking trails to explore.

Slate quarrying on an industrial scale started at Dinorwig in 1809 and reached its peak in the late nineteenth century, when it became one of the greatest quarries in the world, employing over 3,000 workers. The quarry's dramatic slate galleries laid open the side of Elidir mountain, where the 500-million-year-old rock was blasted from the mountainside by explosives. The great slabs of slate were split and dressed to size on the gallery floor, ready for transportation by rail to the harbour at Port Dinorwic and then around the world by sea. Dinorwig produced much of the slate that 'roofed' the Industrial Revolution and continued production until its closure in 1969.

The Vivian Quarry, near the Slate Museum, was named after one of the Dinorwig Quarry managers and its galleries may be clearly seen together with the restored incline down which the slate was carried to the railway. The inclines were powered by gravity, with wagons full of slate travelling down the mountain using their weight to pull up the empty wagons. At the base of the quarry is a sinkhole that once followed the slate vein downwards, but is now filled with water and frequented by sub-aqua divers exploring its depths.

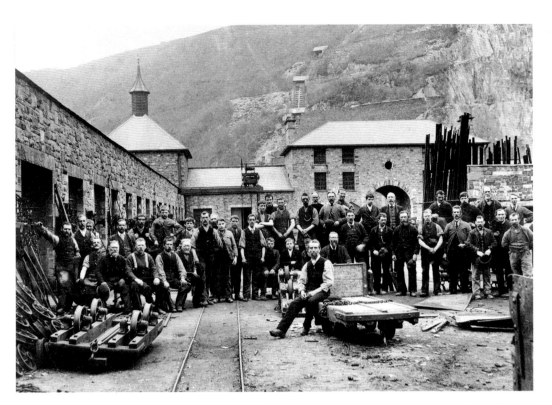

The Dinorwig workshop was a substantial enterprise in itself and the photograph above shows its workforce in 1896. The central figure on the wagon is probably the chief engineer, whose house may be visited at the museum. The machinery at the workshops was driven by water power and the great waterwheel is still preserved on site. The wheel is over 50 feet high and is the largest surviving waterwheel on the British mainland. A rotating line-shaft with drive belts and cogs operated the wide range of machinery in the workshops, including lathes, bellows, hammers, saws and drills. All this may be seen at the museum as well as the foundry and forges, sawmills and loco shed. One of the highlights is a slate-splitting exhibition, a skilled craft illustrated in the old photograph (*right*). The craftsman is using a hammer made of African oak and a wide-bladed chisel, and is sitting on a three-legged sloping stool.

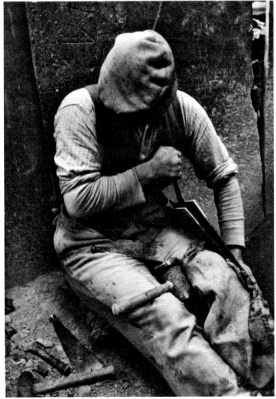

We start our walk in Llanberis High Street, turning left into Capel Goch Road at Joe Brown's Corner Shop (one of the famous climber's shops in Llanberis). We pass the chapel on our left, which bears no less than six dates, the earliest being 1777. Turning right on Fron Goch, we go uphill and take the next left to pass Plas Garnedd Care Centre. The lane climbs upwards, passing through a gate, and as we climb higher there are spectacular views looking back over Llanberis towards Dinorwig Quarry with Llyn Padarn and Llyn Peris appearing. The lane bends around right and becomes a rough track leading up to a ladder stile, after which the path bends back around left and continues alongside a wall. We pass through another gate near the high point of the path, which then levels out, heading west on a clearly defined track. Continuing past a conifer plantation, we pass some old slate tips on our right. The track may be diverted southward here during construction of a proposed hydroelectric scheme but the permanent diversion will be minimal.

As we descend, views open up with the mountains including Moel Eilio and Mynydd Mawr to our left. Mynydd Mawr is known locally as the 'Elephant' due to its distinctive shape. We can see Caernarfon and the Menai Strait ahead, with Anglesey beyond, as the lane continues down towards Waunfawr, bending left to reach a crossroads. On a hill to the right is a building used recently as a climbing centre. This was the location of Marconi's wireless transmitting station that started commercial wireless services across the Atlantic in 1920.

We continue straight ahead at the crossroads for just over half a mile to reach the busy A4085 main road, which, incredibly, was once a quiet village street. The scene pictured below is about 400 metres along the road to our left; the houses on the right are still there, as well as single-storey buildings opposite.

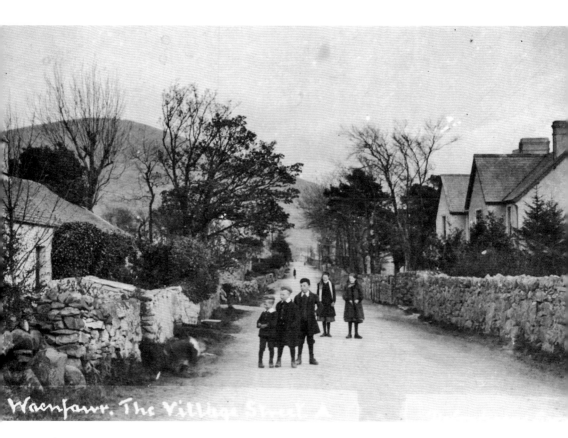

Waunfawr. The Village Street.

46

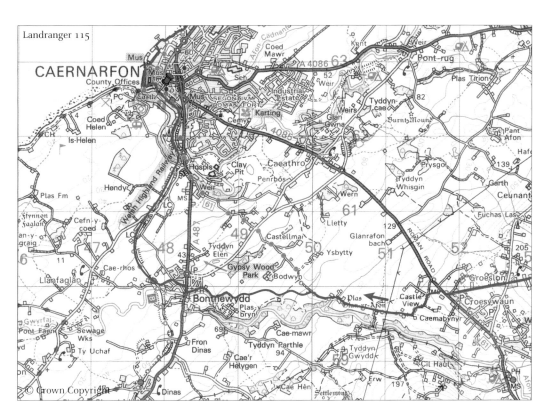

Carefully crossing the main road, we turn right and, after the bus shelter, turn left on a footpath through a kissing gate. The path follows the hedge along, then turns right alongside a low wall to reach another kissing gate and onto a lane, where we turn left. The lane bends a couple of times as we walk through farmland with horses from the nearby riding stables grazing in the fields. It's good to hear the whistle of the Welsh Highland Railway trains as they puff along on the other side of the little valley. Just after Bryn Argoed, the route continues ahead through a gate on the Lôn Gwyrfai cycle track and passes through a farmyard at Plas Glan-yr-Afon, where there are some rather handsome peacocks.

About 250 yards after Ty Gwyn, there's a timber gate on the left with a yellow footpath sign on the post – this footpath sign is easily missed. We turn left here to leave the cycle track and aim for a gap in the wall, where there are two posts standing up. We pass through and turn right as indicated to cross a ladder stile, continuing ahead to cross the field to another ladder stile in the corner. We immediately cross a metal ladder stile to follow the left-hand field edge to yet another ladder stile, continuing ahead before bending left to carry on alongside a wall. The path continues through a metal gate before turning right at a wall corner and through a kissing gate. Bending left through another gate, the path passes a house to reach the Afon Gwyrfai stream, which is followed to Dol Pandy Farm. After passing through a couple of gates to cross the yard, we continue left along the lane, above the river to reach the Newborough Arms in Bontnewydd and some well-earned refreshment.

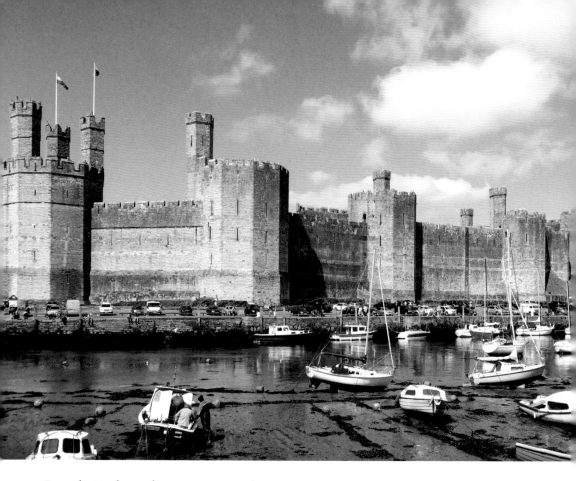

From the Newborough Arms, we turn right along the busy A487 road and cross carefully to turn left along Dol Beuno. The lane bends around left to reach a bridge, where we turn right up to the Welsh Highland Railway track, which we cross with care to join the Lôn Eifion cycle route, turning right. The route follows the left side of the railway and, after crossing the River Seiont, Caernarfon Castle comes into view. The footway passes the railway terminus and continues along the quayside car park, once a busy slate quay. A right turn leads up to the Castle Square, while a walk across the footbridge to the other side of the Seiont is rewarded with a great view of the castle (*above*).

The magnificent castle and town walls are worthy of their World Heritage status and reflect Caernarfon's prestige and strategic importance. The Romans occupied the legionary fort of *Segontium* at Caernarfon for over 300 years and some seven centuries later the Normans built their earth and timber castle beside the Menai Strait. Caernarfon was soon recaptured by the Welsh and was held until the defeat and death of Llywelyn ap Gruffydd in 1282. Edward I then built the great fortress-palace of Caernarfon as a statement of his power, together with his 'iron ring' of castles around North Wales. Edward also ensured that his son, Edward II, the first English Prince of Wales, was born here. The town walls were built at the same time, creating a single entity that has remained largely intact through the centuries. Although the castle was never fully completed, the great angular towers, high battlements and colour-banded walls are said to bear comparison with the imperial walls of Constantinople. A climb to the castle's lofty turrets and a walk around its ramparts are essential to appreciate its majesty.

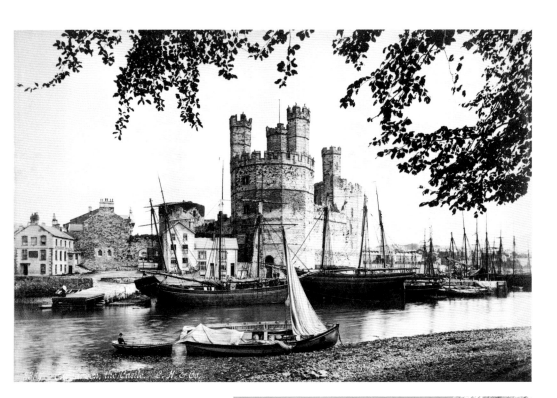

The castle was besieged by Owain Glyndŵr's forces in 1403 and 1404 and was held for the Royalists during the Civil War before it was surrendered to Parliamentary forces in 1646. An order to demolish the castle was fortunately never carried out and much restoration was undertaken in the late nineteenth century. The great Eagle Tower, with its three turrets, dominates the scene above, with sailing vessels moored on the eastern side of the Seiont and along the slate quays. The castle provided the setting for the investitures of the Prince of Wales in 1911 and 1969 and it houses the excellent Regimental Museum of the Royal Welch Fusiliers.

The statue of David Lloyd George (*right*) may be found in Castle Square, beneath the castle walls. Lloyd George was the MP for Carnarvon Boroughs for fifty-five years and became Prime Minister of the United Kingdom during the First World War.

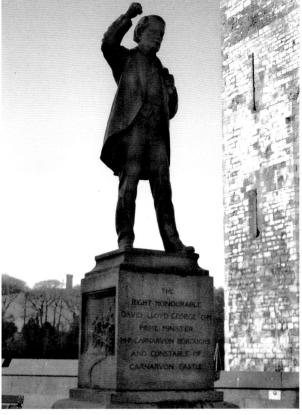

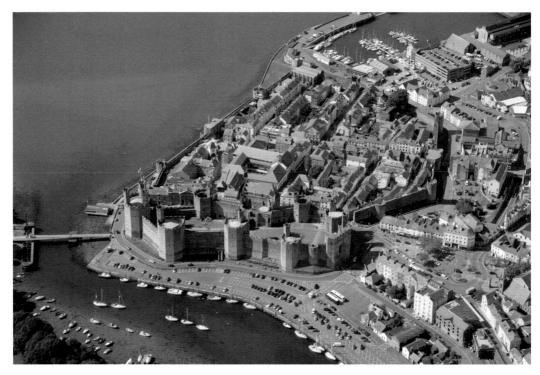

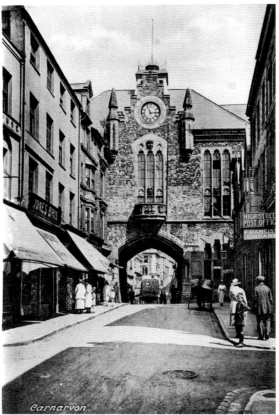

The aerial view above clearly shows the shape of Caernarfon's old town, enclosed by the thirteenth-century town walls and conjoined with the castle. The grid pattern laid out by Edward I can still be seen and the town's High Street crosses from left to right in the centre with gates at each end. At the seaward end is Porth yr Aur (Golden Gate), which now houses the Royal Welsh Yacht Club, and at the town end is Porth Mawr (Great Gate), which was one of the main entrances to the old town. This was protected by a drawbridge in medieval times and the Exchequer was built above the gate. In the eighteenth century this became the Town Hall and later the Guild Hall, seen to the left around the 1930s. It became a cinema and theatre until the 1950s, after which much of the gate building was demolished, but the medieval tower bases still survive.

An exploration of the town is highly recommended and the advice to 'come for the castle, stay for the town' is well meant. During its heyday as a port, Caernarfon is reputed to have had no less than fifty-seven inns and taverns. Inside the town walls, Palace Street was a pub crawler's paradise, having fifteen taverns, while Northgate Street was the heart of the red light district. The street's name in Welsh was Stryd Pedwar a Chwech, which may be translated as 'Four and Six Street'. It's said that visiting sailors could obtain a bed, a bottle of gin and the services of a 'lady of the night' for the sum of four shillings and sixpence! By contrast, along Church Street and incorporated in the corner of the town walls, is the lovely St Mary's church. The church was endowed in the fourteenth century and, although extensively renovated, retains important original features, including the arcades over the nave and the rare Jesse window.

A famous tavern surviving in Northgate Street is the Black Boy Inn (*below*), said to date from 1522. It has walls up to 1½ metres thick and four exterior signs, each showing a 'black buoy' on one side and a 'black boy' on the other. There are several theories to explain the pub's name: one relates to a black boy brought into the country on a ship, while another relates to a navigational buoy that existed in the harbour in the early days of the inn. The pub of today presents an air of respectability very different from the street's notorious past!

Outside the town walls is the bustling Castle Square, once a popular place for cockfighting and bull-baiting, and where the weekly markets have been held since 1284. Lloyd George delivered many of his famous speeches in the Square.

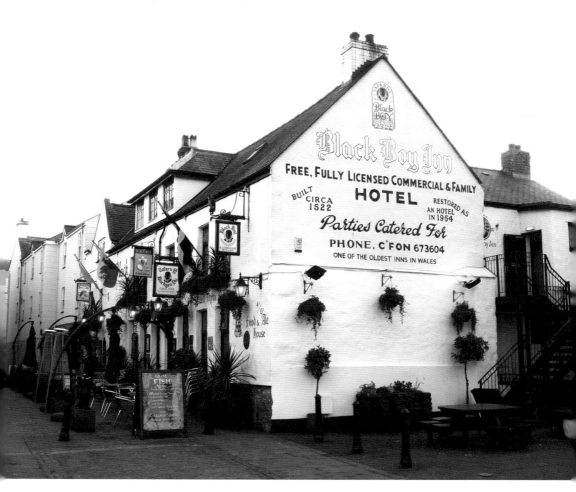

Chapter Six
Caernarfon to Bangor
13.6 miles (21.8 km)

Along the Menai

Today we leave the Royal Town of Caernarfon to follow the Wales Coast Path along the Menai Strait to the City of Bangor. The walk is moderately level and passes the two famous bridges over the Menai with great views across to Anglesey. The route follows the Lôn Las Menai cycle track to Y Felinheli, then leaves the coast to continue on a cycle track and roadside route to the Parc Menai Business Park. From Parc Menai, the Coast Path passes through the Vaynol Estate and the National Trust's Glan Faenol to reach the Britannia Bridge. The path continues alongside the Menai Strait, passing Ynys Gored Goch Island and Telford's Suspension Bridge, eventually arriving at Bangor's Garth Pier. The route then ascends to a pleasant viewpoint and passes some impressive university buildings to reach the centre of Bangor with its historic cathedral. It is hoped that the Coast Path between Y Felinheli and the Britannia Bridge will be diverted nearer the coast in due course, which will avoid the roadside section.

As we leave Caernarfon's town walls and walk around the Victoria Dock, we can reflect on its maritime history. The fine drawing below by Patrick R. Donovan depicts the brig *Cyrus* entering Caernarfon, with the town walls and Eagle Tower in the background. The 132-ton brig was built at Pwllheli in 1837 and was a fast and manoeuvrable merchant vessel.

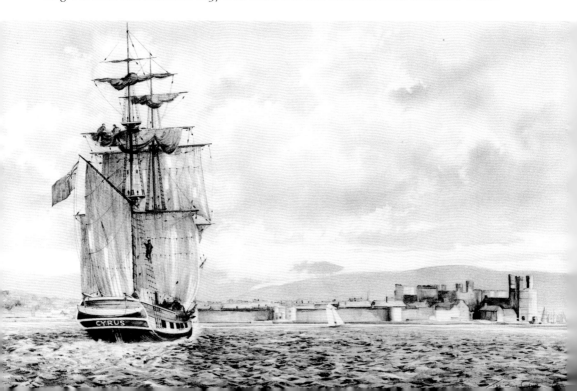

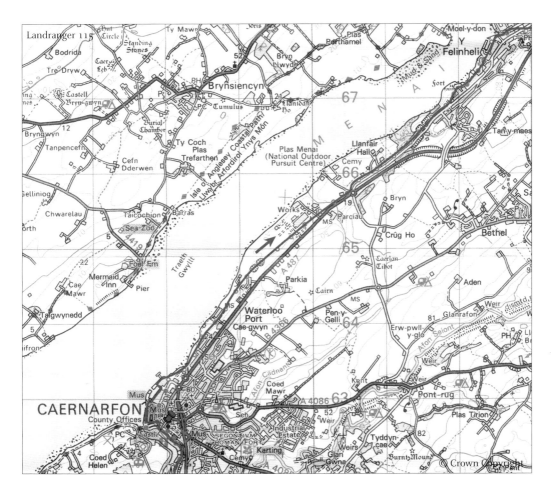

From Victoria Dock we follow the promenade past the Landerne landing pier, continuing around to join the cycle track alongside the Menai. Hopefully, the weather will be kind; the contrasts of the Menai can be appreciated in the lines of 'Night and Morning' by the celebrated Welsh poet R. S. Thomas:

> One night of tempest I arose and went
> Along the Menai shore on dreaming bent;
> The wind was strong, and savage swung the tide,
> And the waves blustered on Caernarfon side.
>
> But on the morrow, when I passed that way,
> On Menai shore the hush of heaven lay;
> The wind was gentle and the sea a flower
> And the sun slumbered on Caernarfon tower.

Our path continues along the Menai, passing 'Yr Hen Erddi', a little garden area with vertical slate slabs bearing interesting Welsh inscriptions. The route carries on between the shore and the road for about 2 miles, passing the old Ferodo works and reaching a roundabout.

The first turning left off the roundabout leads to the Plas Menai National Outdoor Pursuit Centre, but we take the second turning, following the cycle route on the footway alongside the old Caernarfon Road. The road is now much quieter, with the new bypass carrying most of the traffic. After we pass the access to Llanfair Hall, the path veers away from the road a little until we meet a lane with a view of the marina at Y Felinheli ahead. Turning left down the hill we pass through a number of boatyards and marine workshops and along Beach Road towards the village. To the left, there's a pleasant green area and a little promenade with nice views of the Menai. The Moel-y-Don Ferry to Anglesey once operated from here. On our right is the Garddfon Inn, an excellent place for refreshment and full of character, with numerous interesting nautical features.

Around the corner from the inn, the route turns left on a footpath (rather than going up Snowdon Street). It continues past the Port Dinorwic Marina, which is overlooked by some attractive housing along Hen Gei Llechi (the Old Slate Quay). Today's scene is much more tranquil than in times past, when Y Felinheli was known as Port Dinorwic and slate from the Dinorwig Quarries was transported here. The photograph below shows slate being loaded onto the SS *Vaynol* in 1896. The *Vaynol* was built in 1892 as one of the quarry's fleet of steamers that shipped many thousands of tons of slate around the world. Sadly, she was to have a short life; while on a voyage carrying ballast from Glasgow to Port Dinorwic in 1902, she collided with the steamship *Lucerne* off the Mull of Galloway, and sank.

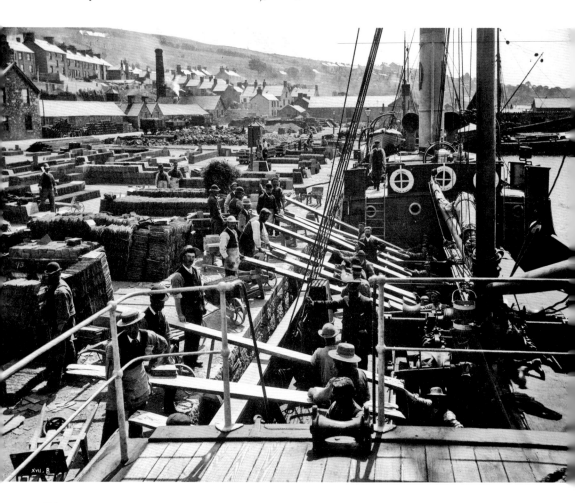

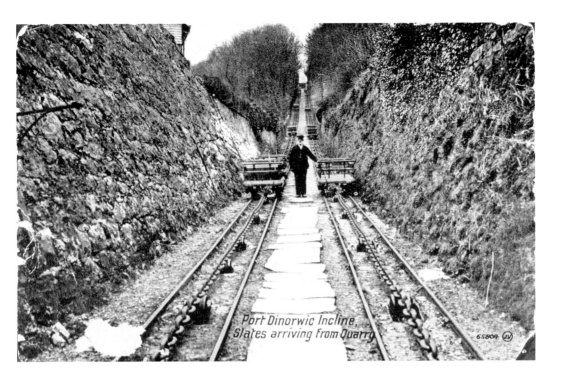

Port Dinorwic Incline,
Slates arriving from Quarry

The route continues around on the footway alongside the inner dock. The building up to the left is the Hotel Port Dinorwic, affectionately known as the 'Pink Palace' due to its exterior colour. Numerous celebrity guests have stayed there over the years, including many television and film personalities.

The slate used to arrive near this point in trucks travelling down the Port Dinorwic Incline (*above*), which connected with the Padarn slate railway from the Dinorwig Quarries. The old slate quays here are now part of the marina and used for leisure (*right*).

There's a bridge to the left that leads to a private estate and it is hoped to divert the Wales Coast Path that way in the future. For now we go up the hill on the footway to reach the main road opposite the Halfway House. We go left, then immediately cross over to follow the cycle track, continuing left along a clear track.

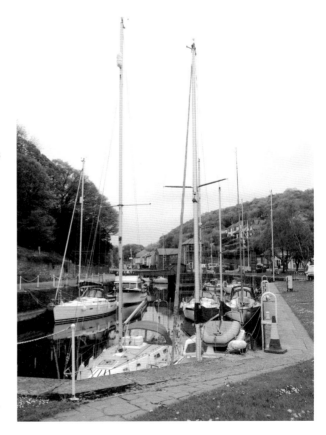

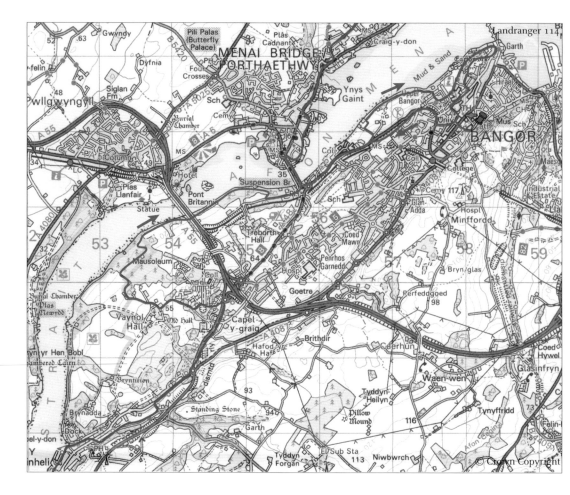

The path passes a bus depot and follows a narrow roadside verge to a junction, where we turn left to reach the B4547 road. Turning right, we follow the footway along the right-hand side, then the left side of the road, passing the imposing entrance to the Vaynol Estate and reaching a roundabout. We take the first exit off the roundabout, following the footway on the right side of the A487 road for just over half a mile. Just before a major roundabout, we cross over to turn left, by the Premier Inn, into Parc Menai Business Park. Walking along Ffordd y Parc, we continue ahead at a roundabout before turning left on Ffordd y Plas along the lane towards the Vaynol Estate buildings. We pass through the farm buildings, continuing on a track and crossing a cattle grid to enter Glan Faenol National Trust property. The path curves around right into a picnic area, which we exit through a gate at the bottom right corner. We turn right on a track here, with the Menai now in view, and bend left, following the edge of the wood. Just after a gate, the path turns right to enter Vaynol Wood, passing a Mausoleum, the family resting place of the Assheton Smiths of Vaynol Estate and owners of the Dinorwig slate quarry. The track curves around left, then there's a little path going off right (easily missed) that leads down through the wood to an ornate gate in the estate wall. The path then follows the Menai shore to the Britannia Bridge.

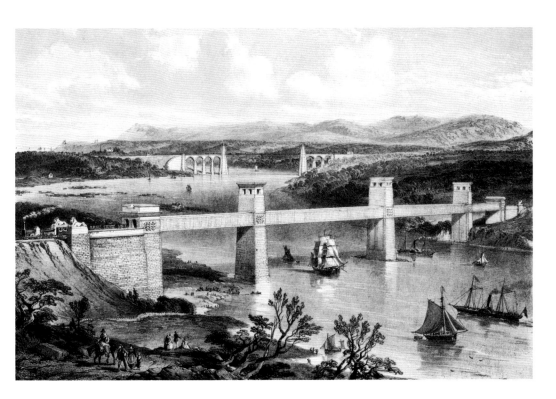

The print above shows the Britannia tubular box-section bridge, built to carry the railway by Robert Stephenson in 1850. Telford's earlier suspension road bridge is in the distance. The Britannia Bridge was badly damaged by fire in 1970 and was rebuilt in two tiers with a road above the railway. The railway reopened in 1972, the road crossing following in 1980.

The photograph below shows the rebuilt, two-level bridge with yachts tacking up the Menai at the start of the 'Round Anglesey' race in 1998. The little island of Ynys Gored Goch can be seen on the left of the picture.

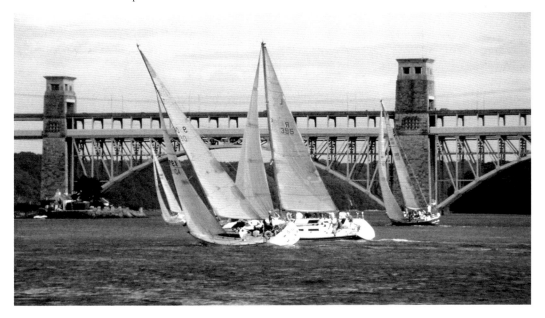

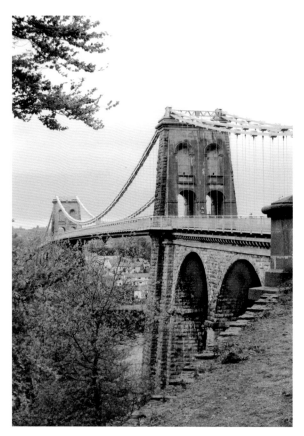

The Coast Path passes under the Britannia Bridge and runs along the shoreline and through Treborth Botanic Garden before turning left along a lane to reach the Menai Suspension Bridge (*left*). The footway passes through an arch in the bridge structure to a roundabout, then continues alongside the main road to reach another roundabout near the Bangor City football stadium. The Coast Path then goes left down a lane and left again, turning right through a kissing gate and taking several lefts and rights before entering woods above the shoreline and eventually reaching a cottage by the shore. There's a 'low-tide' option here, which follows the top of beach, but the regular path leaves the shore to pass up Gorad Road. The route crosses Hwfa Road to a junction where it turns left on Ffordd Siliwen, initially on a footway then along a field path. The path soon rejoins the roadside and continues, with great views, to the Garth Pier (*below*).

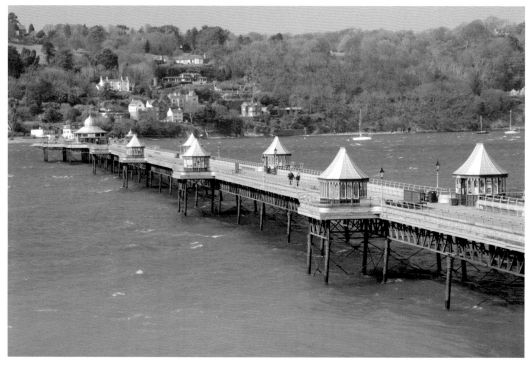

A walk along the magnificent pier is a must and offers great views of the Menai Strait and the Snowdonia hills. The pier dates from 1896 and is over 1,500 feet in length, the second longest in Wales (after Llandudno). It was threatened with demolition in the 1970s but survived thanks to local support and has been beautifully restored.

Our ongoing route passes briefly along Upper Garth Road before turning right on a footpath. The path leads up through trees to the 'Roman Camp' and a viewpoint with a fine outlook over the Menai and Anglesey. Continuing on a track with the university tower visible ahead, we aim for a path in the corner of the wood, forking left, and then right to join the lane at Peacock Walk. This comes out by the BBC Studios, where we turn left, and then right along College Road to walk past some impressive university buildings. We turn left on Penrallt Road, bending around left to pass the University Main Arts Building gate, with its splendid crest. The building's great tower is high above as we turn sharply right, steeply, down the lane. We turn left to the Memorial Arch, crossing over Deiniol Road, then across a pedestrian area, continuing past the cathedral to reach the High Street.

This central location has changed somewhat since Joseph Josiah Dodd painted his *Market Day in Bangor* (*below*) in 1856 – note the profusion of ladies in Welsh costume. There are three taverns in the scene – the Albion Hotel was a busy coaching inn and was visited by George Borrow in 1854. He 'took tea in the immense dining room which was so crowded with guests that its walls literally sweated'. The Castle Hotel was also a posting inn and a high-class hostelry, continuing to be so until its closure in 1989. The Star Inn is the four-storey building next to the Albion Hotel. All three clearly enjoyed a brisk trade on market days!

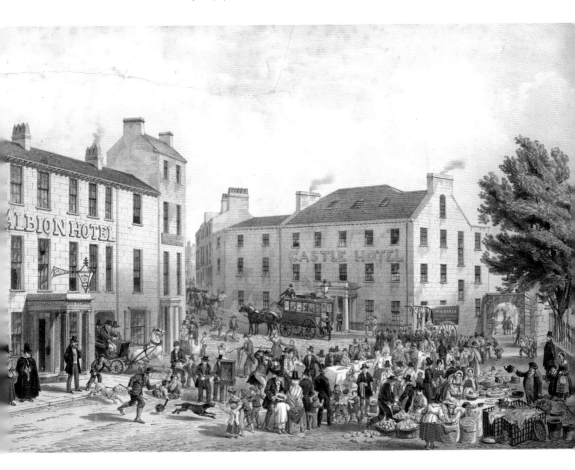

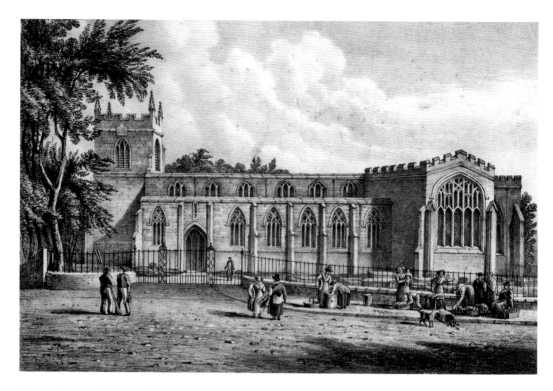

Bangor is one of the smallest cities in Britain, but has a long and rich history. 'Bangor' is an old Welsh word meaning 'enclosure fence' and relates to the site of the present cathedral, where an enclosed monastery was founded by the Celtic saint, Deiniol, around AD 525. When Deiniol was consecrated bishop in 546, his church became a cathedral and Bangor remains the most ancient cathedral site in the country. The cathedral has been built and rebuilt over the centuries, surviving fire and destruction. The Vikings robbed and burned the cathedral in 1073, King John's men destroyed it in 1211 and parts of the cathedral were ravaged during Owain Glyndŵr's revolt in 1402.

Bangor was visited by Gerald of Wales during his journey through the country recruiting for the Third Crusade. He accompanied Baldwin, Archbishop of Canterbury, who celebrated Mass before the high altar in the cathedral on 11 April 1188. Today, the cathedral still has many treasures, including the Mostyn Christ, a celebrated fifteenth-century statue, and the tomb of Owain Gwynedd, Sovereign Prince of Wales, who died in 1169. The charming nineteenth-century print above illustrates Bangor Cathedral's enduring presence at the place where it was founded nearly one and a half millennia ago.

Bangor's High Street is reputed to be the longest in Wales and may be explored in both directions from the cathedral. To the eastern side, there's an interesting 'timeline' of plaques set into the High Street paving that commemorates Bangor's historical events. This passes the city's clock tower and continues in the direction of Porth Penrhyn, Bangor's port, which once handled slate exports from the massive Penrhyn quarries at Bethesda. The great neo-Norman Penrhyn Castle looks down on the port and displays the enormous wealth once generated by the slate and sugar trades.

Chapter Seven
Bangor to Penmon Point
11.4 miles (18.4 km)

Môn Mam Cymru – Mother of Wales

Today we cross the Menai Suspension Bridge to Ynys Môn, the Isle of Anglesey, and walk the Coastal Path to Trwyn Du (Black Point) near Penmon on the island's eastern tip. The walk is fairly easy going, with a few short hills, and passes through Upper Bangor before crossing over Telford's spectacular bridge to reach the town of Menai Bridge (Porthaethwy). The path leaves the coast to pass the village of Llandegfan, with great views across the Menai, then rejoins the shore at the attractive town of Beaumaris, with its superb castle and pier. The walk continues on the coastal path to Lleiniog then visits Penmon and the ancient priory before finally arriving at Trwyn Du with its lighthouse and view of Puffin Island.

The route from Bangor Cathedral returns towards the Memorial Arch, with a view ahead of the University Main Arts Building and its tower (*below*). The university was founded in 1884 by public subscription including voluntary contributions from local farmers and quarrymen. It was originally based in an old coaching inn at Penrhyn, having just fifty-eight students and ten members of staff. The splendid Main Building was opened by King George V in 1911 and today, Bangor University has over 12,000 students and 2,000 staff and is a world leader in research and teaching.

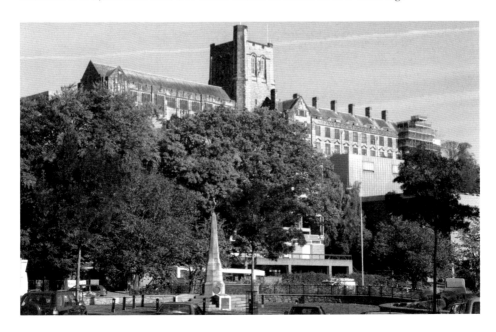

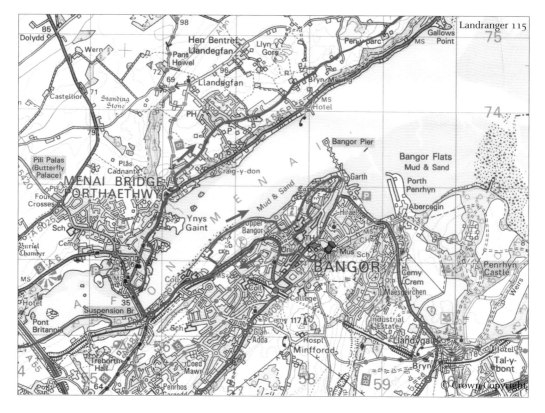

The Bangor War Memorial shown in the previous photograph is devoted to local people who fell in both World Wars, while the imposing North Wales Heroes' Memorial Arch on the other side of Deiniol Road commemorates all those from North Wales who fell in the First World War. Alongside the Memorial Arch, Bangor's new arts and innovation centre, Pontio, is due to open in 2014.

Passing the Memorial Arch, we turn steeply left up Glanrafon Hill, forking right to reach the main Holyhead Road at Upper Bangor. Turning right, we pass some shops and cross the main road to the footway on the left side, following the bend around left. Just after the junction with Menai Avenue, there's a footpath veering to the left, which parallels the main road through a wooded area for about half a mile. The upper of two paths is preferred, away from the noise of the main road. The path eventually drops down to rejoin the road and we cross over to follow the footway on the right side for about two thirds of a mile to the Menai Suspension Bridge. There are footways on both sides of the bridge crossing – the one on the right side offers better views and we can see part of our ongoing route on the Anglesey shore.

Thomas Telford's magnificent iron suspension bridge opened in 1826 and was the first of its kind in the world. The bridge provided an important link in the London to Holyhead route to Ireland; previously, the traffic had to be carried across the Menai by ferries that were notoriously unreliable. The bridge's great towers were constructed from Penmon limestone, floated from the quarries by sea and its sixteen iron chains each weighed 25 tons. When their lifting was finally achieved, the successful operation was celebrated with 'plenty of ale'!

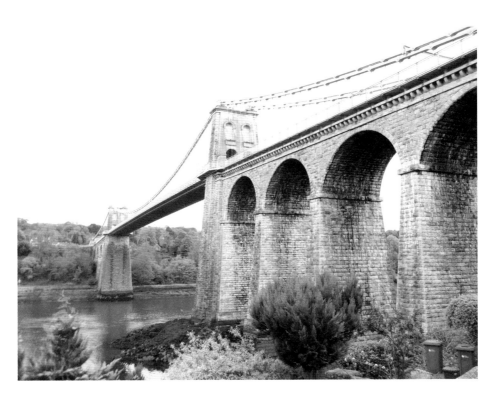

After crossing the bridge, we turn back right by the Bridge Inn, then fork right on Cambria Road, going down to meet the Anglesey Coastal Path. There's a viewing area back below the bridge that offers an impression of its great scale (*above*).

The bridge was designed to have a clearance of 100 feet above high water to allow the passage of high-masted sailing ships, as seen in the print of 1840 below. There are four piers on the Anglesey side and three on the mainland side.

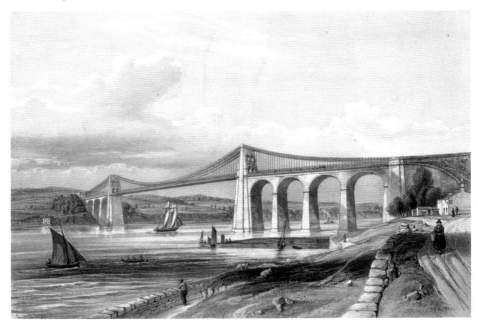

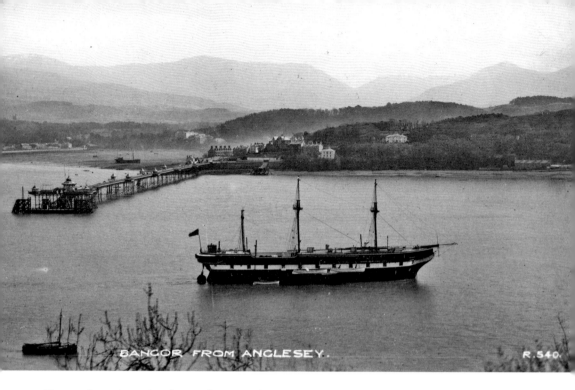

BANGOR FROM ANGLESEY.

R.540.

The Anglesey Coastal Path runs for 125 miles around the island and the excellent Official Guide by Carl Rogers describes the entire route in detail. The concise directions included here will enable our part of the route to be followed without difficulty, particularly as the path is well waymarked with the distinctive 'sandwich tern' logo.

From Cambria Road, the path continues left, then turns right by the Liverpool Arms to pass through blue gates to the promenade and St George's Pier. The path then goes through a gate and turns right along St George's Road, continuing up to reach the main A545 road, where we turn right. The road passes a couple of islands and crosses a bridge over a tidal creek, after which the route turns left steeply up the lane to Llandegfan. This is quieter than the main road and it is pleasant passing Llandegfan village, with views across the Menai towards Bangor and the Snowdonia hills.

The photograph above of the view towards Bangor in 1917 recalls the time when the 'school' ship HMS *Clio* was stationed in the Menai. She was a 22-gun corvette that had seen naval service in the Pacific and Australia before becoming an industrial training ship in 1877. She served a dual purpose as a reformatory school for delinquent boys and a training facility for future seamen. Life on board was harsh but many of the boys went on to find regular employment, many of them in the armed services. Inevitably, a number of the 260 boys on board lost their lives whilst serving on *Clio*, either from disease or accidents, such as falling from the rigging. There are five headstones in Llandegfan church cemetery bearing the names of twenty-nine *Clio* boys.

The lane continues ahead, becoming narrower then, where it swings around left. We go ahead over a stile to reach a kissing gate and then angle left across the field to follow the marker posts through the gorse and past Pen-y-parc house.

The path continues down the driveway of Pen-y-parc to turn right on a lane known as 'Allt Gôch Bach', which is followed down past the golf club with good views towards Penmon Point and the Great Orme. The lane joins the A545 main road and we cross to follow the footway alongside into Beaumaris, enjoying the views along the seafront. The route enters the town on the main street, which is Castle Street. This leads on towards the castle, but just after the Liverpool Arms Hotel, the Coastal Path turns right on Alma Street to follow around to Beaumaris Pier.

The charming picture below shows Beaumaris Pier in 1906 with the paddle steamer *La Margeurite* alongside and a Hackney cab waiting to pick up the travellers. It is pleasant to walk on today's redeveloped pier to enjoy the scenery and to look at the interesting landing pontoon at the seaward end.

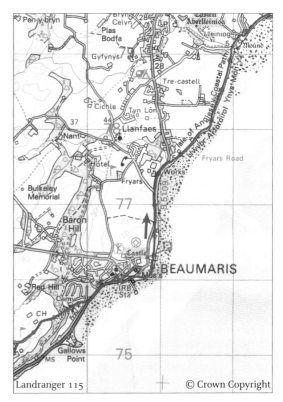

Landranger 115   © Crown Copyright

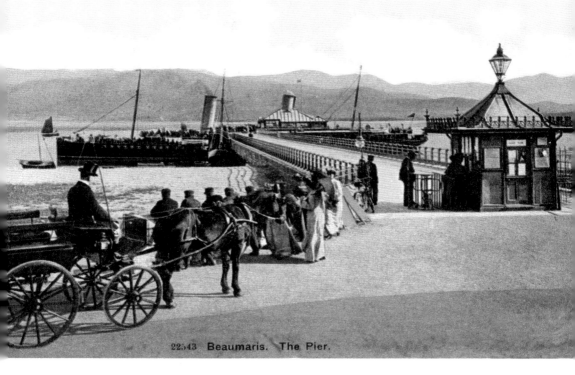

22543 Beaumaris. The Pier.

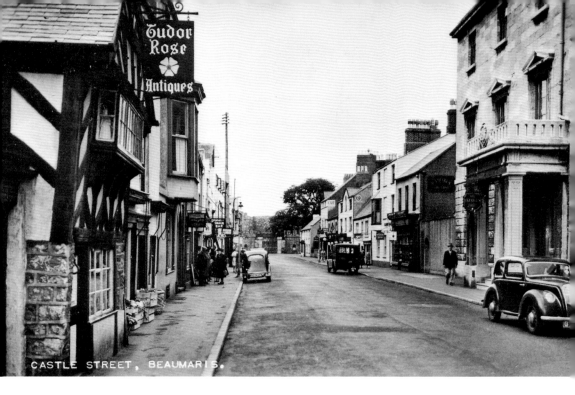

CASTLE STREET, BEAUMARIS.

A good exploration of Beaumaris is essential and an ideal place to start is Beaumaris Gaol, which offers an insight into conditions 'behind bars' in earlier times. The condemned cell and the treadwheel may be seen, as well as the place where hangings took place on a platform above the street. The last man to be hanged there in 1862 put a curse on the church clock opposite the scaffold and it has not kept time ever since!

The church of St Mary and St Nicholas was built mainly in the fourteenth century. It holds a royal tomb much older than the church itself, that of Princess Joan, daughter of King John of England, who married Llywelyn Fawr, Prince of Wales, and who died in 1237.

The town's main street, Castle Street, is pictured above in the 1950s. The Tudor Rose building is reputedly the town's oldest townhouse, while the portico opposite is the entrance to the splendid Bulkeley Hotel, named after the prominent Beaumaris family, who were responsible for building it. The hotel's main entrance faces the seafront and it has welcomed many celebrated guests, including Queen Victoria in 1851. It has an amiable ghost called 'George'!

Castle Street leads to the town's old courthouse, where many of the gaol's prisoners would have received their sentences, and then on to the famous castle. Beaumaris was the last of Edward I's great chain of castles, built to stamp out the resistance of the Welsh. Its level site allowed it to be built on a concentric 'walls-within-walls' design with perfect symmetry. It has four rings of impregnable defence, including the moat, and could be supplied directly from the sea by a tidal dock, which allowed ships to sail right up to the castle. It was begun in 1295 but work ceased in 1330 before its towers reached their full height. It was sufficiently complete, however, to be garrisoned and besieged during Owain Glyndŵr's revolt.

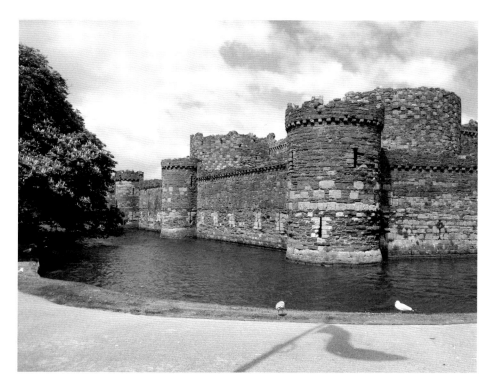

The 'ruinous and decayed' castle was renovated by Viscount Bulkeley in the Royalist cause in the Civil War but was surrendered to the Parliamentarian Maj.-Gen. Thomas Mytton in 1646. Today's castle (*above*) is much as it was in 1330 and is now cared for by Cadw.

The castle viewed from the north (*below*) doesn't dominate the skyline with tall towers, but sits contentedly, facing the sea and the mountains, an enduring presence in the landscape.

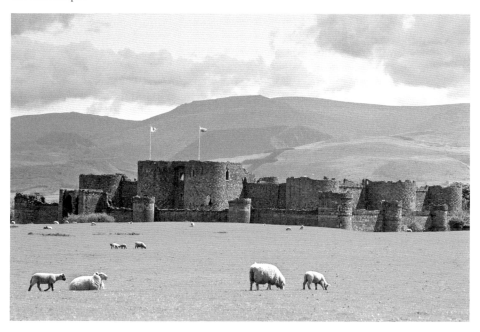

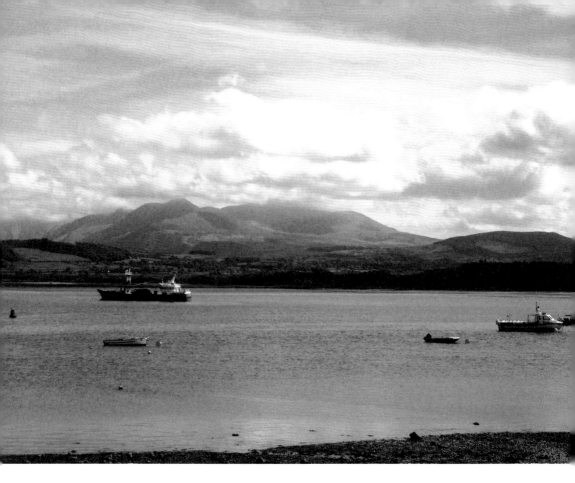

From Beaumaris Pier, the Coastal Path turns right to the Lifeboat House, continuing left along the promenade and passing a stone circle in front of the imposing Victoria Terrace. The path continues along a superb grassy section with a great view of the Menai and Snowdon mountains (*above*), then joins the footway alongside the road, continuing along the seashore and passing the turning to Llanfaes. The footway and verge are very narrow here and the beach is preferable if the tides allow.

Just past the Llanfaes turning, there's a wide slipway that was linked with the Saunders Roe Factory on the other side of the road. The factory modified Catalina flying boats during the Second World War and its old buildings are visible to the left.

The official route joins the beach where the road bends left and, if the tide is low or falling, it may be followed along the beach to Lleiniog. High tides cover much of the beach and reach right up to the cliffs, so the walk along the shore to Lleiniog and Trwyn y Penrhyn must not be attempted within one hour either side of high tide, particularly if there is a strong onshore wind. It takes about forty minutes to complete this section. If there is any doubt, the lanes inland should be taken, following the signs to Penmon Priory (*see maps on pages 65 & 71*).

The walk along the beach is delightful and in just over a mile reaches a stream and picnic area at Lleiniog. We turn left here to join the lane where we turn right and after a short distance, right again to return to the beach (depending on the tide). At the end of the small bay, we reach a ramp and embankment and rejoin the lane to follow it to Penmon Priory.

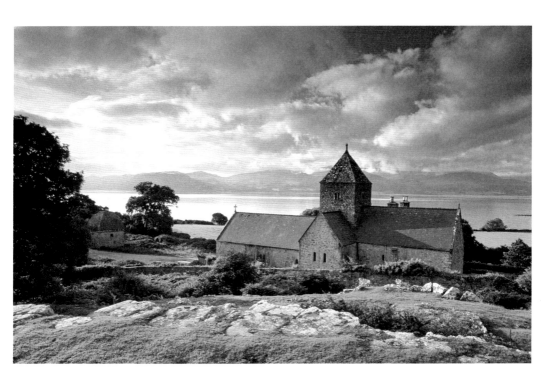

Penmon Priory (*above*) is the site of a monastery founded in the sixth century by St Seiriol, whose holy well may be found nearby. The church was rebuilt in the twelfth century before becoming an Augustinian priory, when further monastic buildings were added. The two finely carved tenth-century crosses inside the church are of particular interest.

At the Dissolution, the priory became the property of the Bulkeley family, who built the elegant dovecot opposite. The dovecot (*right*) has about 930 nesting holes and the young pigeons provided a source of tender meat. The pigeons could fly in and out through the cupola above the roof.

Penmon limestone was quarried from land nearby and was much prized for building. It was used at Beaumaris Castle and both bridges across the Menai Strait.

From Penmon Priory, the road is followed to the end of the headland at Trwyn Du (Black Point) where there's a small café and toilets open during summer.

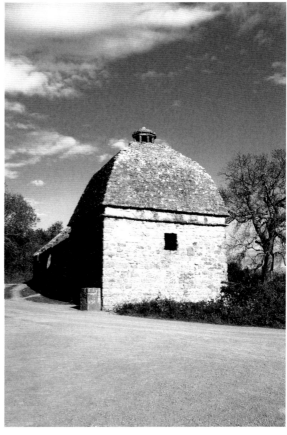

Chapter Eight

Penmon Point to Moelfre

13.8 miles (22.2 km)

Arthur's Table and the Red Wharf

Today's route continues along the Anglesey Coastal Path and is a strenuous day's walking, with lots of 'rise and fall', although it may be divided at several points if so wished. The first section to Red Wharf Bay is not truly coastal, and follows paths and lanes inland, but is very pleasant and reaches an airy hilltop at Bwrdd Arthur, the site of an Iron Age hill fort that affords views across the wide expanse of Red Wharf Bay. The next section follows the top of the beach around the bay with the Ship Inn beckoning in the far distance. After some welcome refreshment, the path is followed around to the popular resort of Benllech before rising to pass along dramatic limestone cliffs to reach Traeth Bychan. A final short section leads to the attractive fishing village of Moelfre, with its renowned lifeboat station.

At our starting point at Trwyn Du there's a good view of the lighthouse and Puffin Island (*below*). The lighthouse has marked the passage between the two islands since 1838 and was welcomed following a disaster seven years earlier when the paddle steamer *Rothsay Castle* was wrecked nearby with the loss of over 100 lives. Puffin Island (Ynys Seiriol) has the remains of a monastic settlement that was once a sister foundation to that of Penmon.

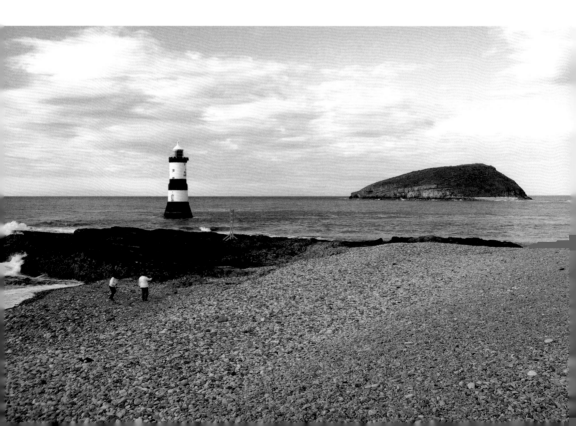

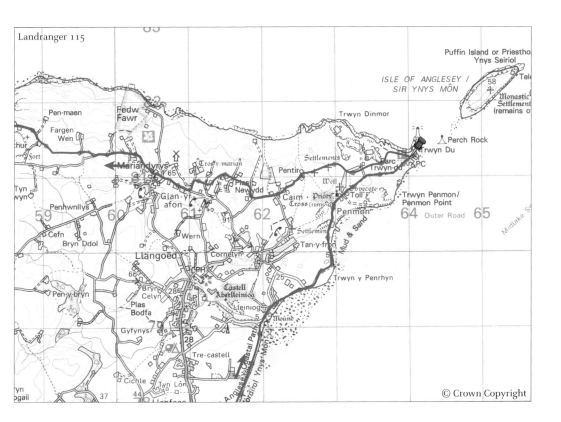

© Crown Copyright

The official Coastal Path goes off left just before the point at Trwyn Du, but there's a footpath closer to the sea, which may be followed for a short distance. This turns left where it says 'No Access – Quarry Workings', and rejoins the main Coastal Path, where we turn right. We reach a lane and follow the waymarks, continuing alongside a long wall with some interesting stone projections. This leads to Pentir Cottage, where we join a lane that bends a couple of times before continuing straight ahead, passing a junction. The path then turns right off the lane down a private drive to turn left just before a cream house, through a kissing gate. The well waymarked path meanders through several gates and between some attractive buildings at Pen Marian Mawr to reach a little triangle in the lanes, which is passed to a kissing gate. The ongoing path eventually reaches a lane where we turn right to reach a T-junction just north of Glan-yr-afon village. There's a great view looking back over the Menai Strait towards the mountains as we turn right to continue up the lane.

The Coastal Path follows the lane, past the Ty Newydd entrance and a little chapel. Soon after the chapel there's a stile and gate on the right, where we turn right. This is the access drive to Fargen Wen and when it swings right we continue ahead down a grassy path. The path follows a couple of field edges before skirting around the north side of Bwrdd Arthur hill fort, passing a house at Ty-mawr and reaching the farm at Tan-dinas. About 200 metres after the farm there's a track curving left around the western side of Bwrdd Arthur. This is the current route of the Coastal Path, diverted due to landslip on the next section.

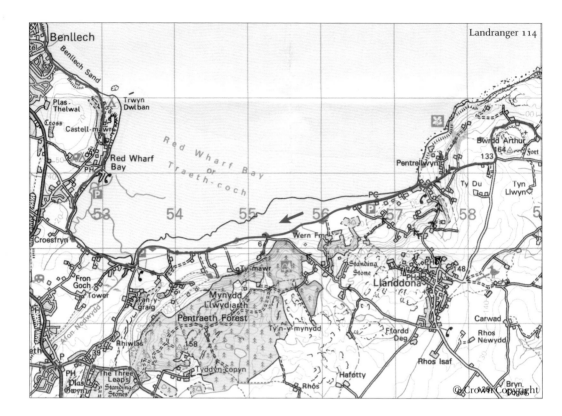

The curving track rises to meet a stile, and to visit the top of Bwrdd Arthur, there's a path on the left, just before the stile, that goes up through the gorse to the trig point on the summit. Bwrdd Arthur means 'Arthur's Table' and the distinctive flat-topped hill can be seen for miles around. The hill fort is known as Din Sylwy and is one of the largest hill forts in Anglesey, probably dating from the Iron Age. It was occupied in the Romano-British period and has yielded finds, including Roman pottery and coins and earlier Iron Age artefacts. The limestone-walled settlement is roughly oval in shape and its position is commanding. The view towards Red Wharf Bay shows our way forward.

The stile leads onto a lane where we turn right, and then right again just before the transmitter station, down the lane known as Lôn Goch. The lane is steep and narrow and gets very busy at holiday time but Red Wharf Bay is a great sight ahead. The lane goes around right by the little church of St Dona to reach the beach road, which we follow along, passing the Llanddona car park. Where the road bends left, the Coastal Path turns right, behind the beach, to continue on an elevated sea wall across a marshy area. After the sea wall, a lane entrance is passed; if the tide is high, a public path may be followed through Pentraeth Forest, otherwise we can continue walking along the back of the beach, enjoying the beautiful scenery (*opposite*). This is a huge bay and the Ship Inn in the distance is a tempting target. The path eventually reaches a parking area, which is exited over a stone bridge and then turns right to cross another bridge over the Afon Nodwydd stream.

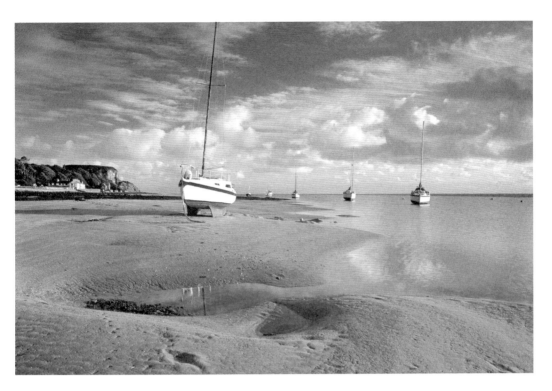

The path continues around the marshy western end of the bay and this section can be walked at all times except for one hour either side of high tide. The path leaves the shore at Porth-llongdy-uchaf to go briefly up a lane before turning right through a kissing gate to follow a little path through the trees and reaching the Ship Inn at Red Wharf Bay (Traeth-coch). The inn is pictured below across the little harbour around the 1930s.

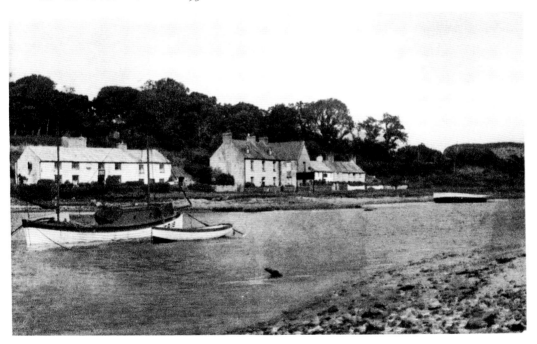

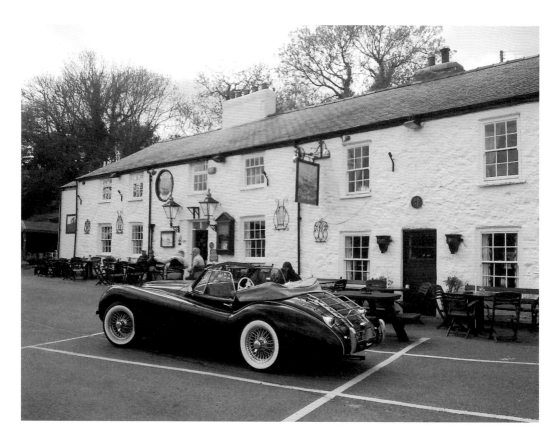

The Ship Inn, shown above with a superb Jaguar sports car outside, has an interesting history. The pub was once known as the Little Quay and, later, the Old Quay, and was frequented by sailors bringing their cargoes of coal and other goods to the port in their sailing ships. The little port was evidently a busy place, with exports including grain and minerals. Shipbuilding also took place here, but on a fairly small scale. The little harbour now provides shelter for small yachts and pleasure craft and the Ship's customers are now likely to include the yachtsmen and visitors enjoying the magnificent outlook across the bay.

Red Wharf Bay has seen its share of shipwrecks, including a brig, believed to be the *Maria*, wrecked during the Great Gale of 25/26 October 1859, which saw the loss of very many vessels and lives around western coasts, including the *Royal Charter* at Moelfre (*see Chapter Nine*).

Our walk continues along the coast from the Ship Inn, passing the lane on the left and continuing along the shore past the sailing club entrance and along a driveway before curving sharply around left. The path ascends then turns right and the huge limestone rock to the right, facing the sea is known as Castell-mawr. The engraving opposite by William Daniell, published in 1815, shows the quarrying of Black Marble at Red Wharf Bay. The quarry was probably near Castell-mawr and the quay may be seen in the background, with sailing ships loading. The hill in the distance looks like Bwrdd Arthur.

By a gate marked 'Private', the path turns left with caravans on either side to turn right alongside the caravan site access road, keeping left as waymarked and forking right to pass behind the clubhouse then turning left just before the beach.

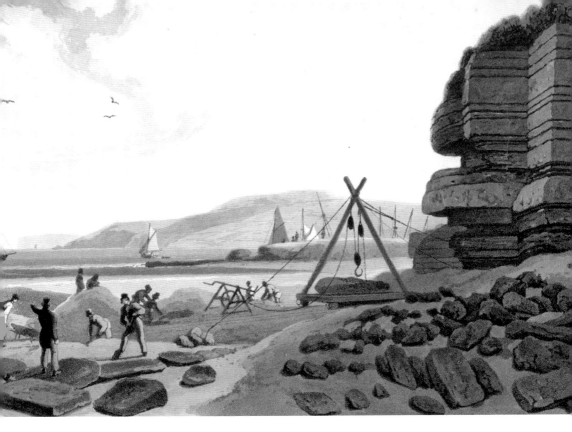

This is a pleasant path, just above the beautiful beach of Benllech Sand, and we follow it along to reach the road and turn right to walk down the hill to the promenade. The postcard below shows Benllech Promenade in the 1940s, when cars were available in any colour as long as it was black. Spot the exception!

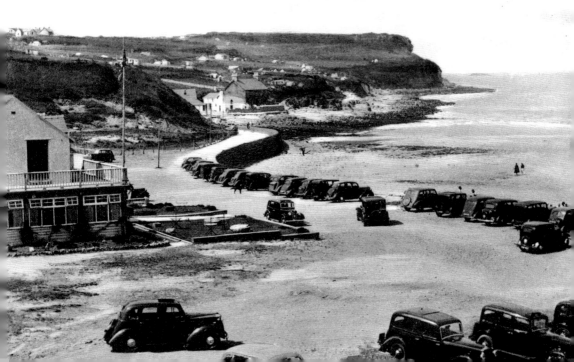

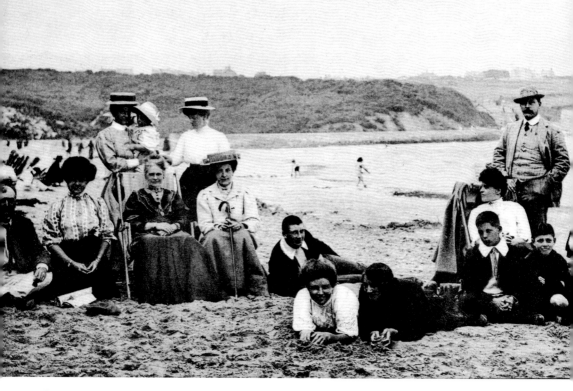

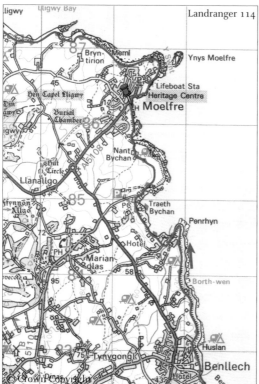

Benllech, with its lovely sandy beach and great outlook, is one of the most popular holiday places on the island. It was clearly much enjoyed by families in Edwardian times, as shown by the well-dressed beach group (*above*) posing in 1909.

After strolling along the promenade, we continue on the Coastal Path by turning right opposite Ffordd Cynlas, down some steps, by a little stream. The path then climbs steeply to follow the top of the cliffs, passing a caravan site. The path runs close to the edge of the cliffs along here, so care is needed. We can look back across Benllech Sand towards Red Wharf Bay and Bwrdd Arthur with Puffin Island in the distance. In the far distance we can see the Great Orme and the mountains of Snowdonia.

As we follow the waymarkers around the headland at Penrhyn, we can see Traeth Bychan ahead and Moelfre with its lifeboat station in the distance.

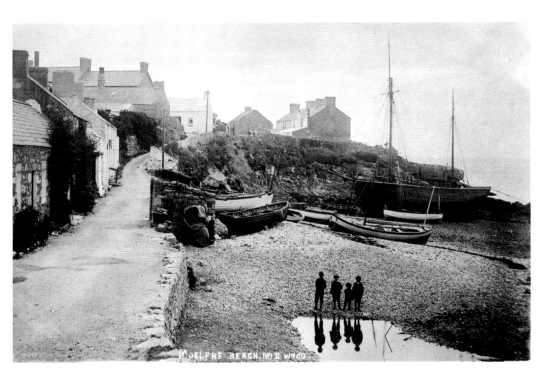

We pass some attractive chalets and continue ahead alongside a little stream, eventually passing caravans and turning right after a gate to drop down to cross the back of Traeth Bychan beach. At low tides, the route continues along the beach otherwise, for three hours each side of high tide, the path leads up some steps to cross a couple of fields behind a caravan site to drop down to a car park at the northern end of the beach. From here, the path turns right and continues up through fields to reach Nant Bychan farmyard, continuing right along the access lane and turning right to reach the back of the shingle beach at Porth yr Aber. From here the Coastal Path continues to Moelfre, turning right down the hill to reach the village's pebble beach.

Moelfre is a picturesque fishing village and its maritime past is shown in the photograph of the beach above, dating from around 1910. The picture is taken from the freshwater pool and the reflections of the little boys are captured perfectly, with the fishing boats and two-masted schooner adding to the atmosphere of the scene.

People from Moelfre have sailed all over the world and among these was Thomas Lewis 'Twm Pen Stryd', who was one of only three sailors to survive the *Cospatrick* disaster in 1874. The emigrant ship was sailing to New Zealand with 473 passengers and crew aboard including 429 emigrants, many of them women and children. She caught fire south of the Cape of Good Hope and what followed was a harrowing story. Despite desperate efforts to extinguish the fire, the ship sank and almost all were drowned. One overloaded lifeboat capsized, another disappeared and the last lifeboat was left floating without food or water for ten days. When the ship *British Sceptre* finally picked up the survivors, only five were left alive, having resorted to cannibalism. Two of these had 'gone mad' and died shortly afterwards.

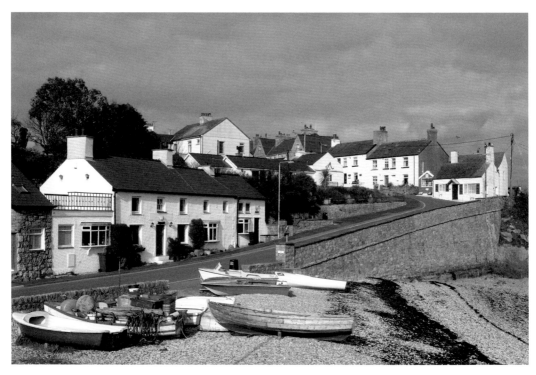

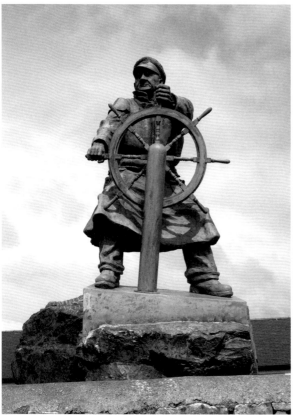

Moelfre (*above*) has centuries
of maritime history with many
tales of bravery and disaster. The
Moelfre lifeboat has played a major
part in the village's proud record
and has participated in many
rescues since its establishment in
1848. Countless lives have been
saved by the crew, who have
selflessly risked their own lives to
save others.

The tragic story of the *Royal
Charter* is related in the next
chapter, but exactly 100 years after
this disaster, the MV *Hindlea* was
wrecked close to the same rocks
near Moelfre in a hurricane storm
on 27 October 1959. The lifeboat
crew, led by Coxswain Richard
'Dic' Evans, courageously rescued
the *Hindlea*'s crew of eight before
she was destroyed on the rocks.
Coxswain Evans received the
RNLI's highest gold medal award
for his part in the rescue, the first
of two such awards he received. His
inspiring statue (*left*) may be seen
alongside the Seawatch Centre.

Chapter Nine
Moelfre to Amlwch Port
12.0 miles (19.3 km)

The Copper and the Gold

This is quite a strenuous walk on the Coastal Path, with plenty of height gain and loss, but there's much of interest along the route. The walk passes the Seawatch Centre and lifeboat station before visiting the *Royal Charter* memorial. It then passes attractive beaches at Traeth Lligwy and Traeth yr Ora before turning inland to follow around the Traeth Dulas Estuary, passing the welcoming Pilot Boat Inn. The path returns to follow a rugged but beautiful section of coast, passing the lighthouse at Point Lynas and continuing along the cliffs to reach Amlwch Port, with its fascinating history of copper trading and shipbuilding.

From Moelfre seafront, our path goes right, around to the Seawatch Centre, a museum and shop celebrating Anglesey's rich maritime history. The statue of Coxswain Evans here was unveiled by HRH The Prince of Wales in 2004. The path passes the lifeboat station to turn left across a small shingle beach and follow the coast around to Porth Helaeth Bay. Just after Porth Helaeth, on a rise to the left, is the *Royal Charter* memorial stone.

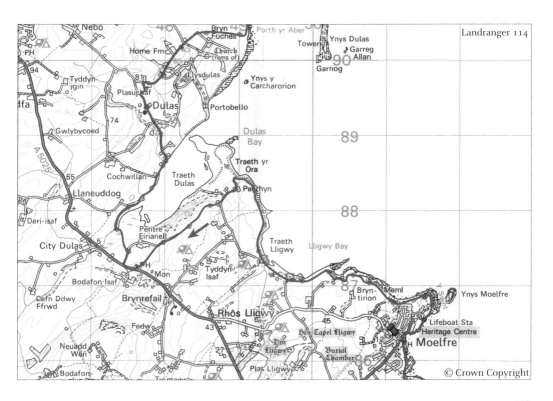

Landranger 114

© Crown Copyright

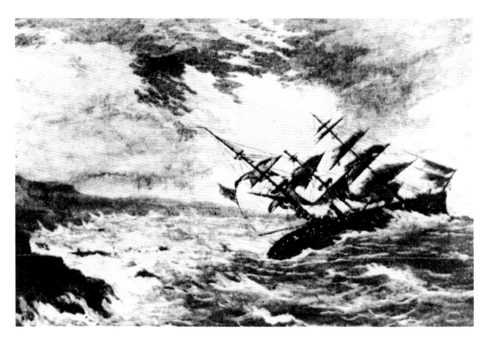

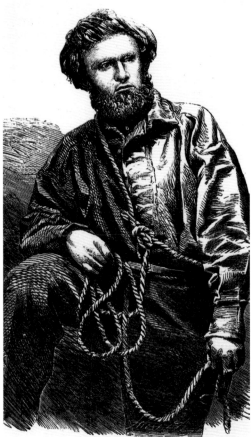

JOSEPH RODGERS, SEAMAN, OF THE "ROYAL CHARTER."

The *Royal Charter* left Melbourne on 26 August 1859 and was virtually at the end of her long voyage to Liverpool. She had been built in 1856 and was one of a new class of vessels with steam engines to supplement her sails, able to complete the Australia to Liverpool run in record time. She was in sight of her destination but tragically became caught in the great hurricane on the night of 25/26 October 1859 (*above*). With both anchors parted she was driven to destruction on the rocks near Porth Helaeth. She was carrying 112 officers and crew and over 350 passengers, many returning from the Australian goldfields. It's estimated that several millions of pounds worth of gold (at today's values) went down with the ship. In the raging storm there was little that could be done to rescue anyone and over 400 people sadly lost their lives. One of the crew, the Maltese sailor 'Joe Rogers' (*left*), heroically managed to get a line ashore, and a bosun's chair was rigged, saving sixteen crewmen. The ship was breaking up, however, and few others survived despite the brave efforts of the local community.

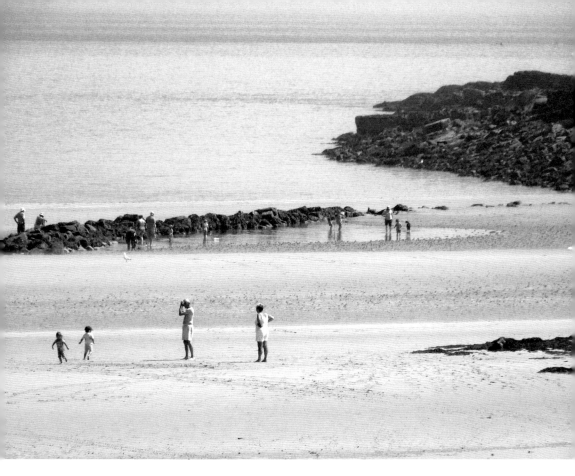

The wreckage from the *Royal Charter* was strewn over the rocks and the following days and weeks saw the gruesome task of recovering the bodies as well as an unseemly scrabble to salvage the gold. The disaster touched the whole country and Charles Dickens visited the scene shortly afterwards, writing of his experiences in his book *The Uncommercial Traveller*. Many of those who died are buried locally.

The path continues along the coast to the beach of Traeth Lligwy. At the right-hand end of the beach there's an ancient 'fish weir' (*above*), built on a crescent of rocks that become visible at low tide. The weir is submerged at high tide and was used to trap fish in the pond created when the tide goes out.

When we reach the lovely sandy cove of Traeth yr Ora, our path turns left, away from the coast, and goes to Penrhyn farm, where we turn right to continue up a track, turning right around a cottage garden then left, as waymarked, through a kissing gate and into fields. There's a good view of the Traeth Dulas Estuary down to the right and the track eventually arrives at a pond that has a fence going right through the middle! Skirting around the side of the pond, the hedge is regained, leading to a gate in the corner, after which we follow the waymarked track ahead. Where this bears right, we cross the stile directly ahead to follow the field edge to the Pilot Boat Inn. It has been suggested that this last section of path leading from the coast is an old smugglers' route. Perhaps some of the contraband found its way into the cellars of the Pilot Boat Inn. Anyway, the inn is a good place to rest after the first section of our day's walk.

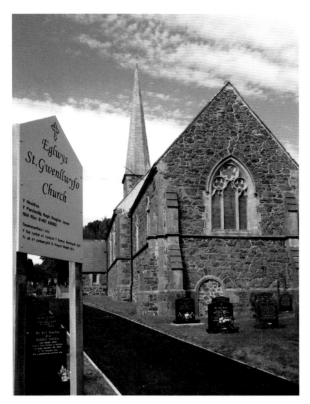

From the Pilot Boat Inn, we follow the main road for about 150 metres before turning right down a farm access road then going left through a kissing gate to reach a footbridge. The path bends around right, down the side of the estuary, crossing a marshy area and turning right on a lane which becomes a tidal track that floods at high tide. It's great walking along the sand and looking out over Traeth Dulas with its wreck of an old wooden fishing boat. It's a shame to leave the shore to turn left up a tarmac lane.

The lane passes the little church of St Gwenllwyfo (*left*), which has its place in the story of the Amlwch Riots of 1817. The riots were caused by a number of factors: there was high unemployment in Anglesey due to many soldiers returning from the Napoleonic Wars and a poor grain harvest had led to widespread hunger and poverty.

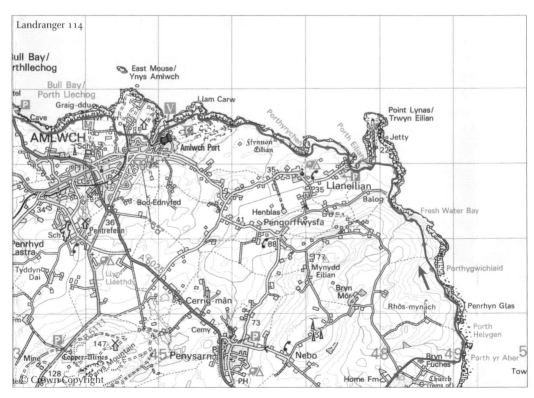

There was great anger that a ship called the *Wellington* was loaded with precious Anglesey corn in Amlwch Port, bound for England where there were those who could afford to pay for it. People on Anglesey were starving and efforts were made to prevent the *Wellington* from sailing with the grain. In the dead of night, her rudder was stolen and hidden at Llanwenllwyfo church, 3 miles from Amlwch. The authorities then arrested three of the protest's ringleaders, one of whom was imprisoned in Beaumaris Gaol. The street protests continued and a detachment of troops had to be sent from Ireland to control the situation. Order was eventually restored and the rudder was discovered and returned to the ship, but the hardship of the people had been clearly demonstrated. A series of relief efforts and public works later helped to defuse the unrest.

About 200 metres after the church, the path turns right through a kissing gate, following the field edge around to another kissing gate and onto a lane, where we turn right to pass Home Farm on our left. At a T-junction, we go straight ahead over a ladder stile, continuing to another ladder stile where we bear half right. The path continues down to the coast following the right edge of several fields, eventually reaching the bottom fence at Porth yr Aber, where we turn left.

There's a good view here of the island of Ynys Dulas, a kilometre or so offshore. Its distinctive tower was built in the 1820s to store food and provide refuge for shipwrecked seamen. The island is now a home for seals and seabirds.

The Coastal Path continues on its undulating route, with helpful marker posts, passing several coves, including the lovely Porthygwichiaid (Periwinkle Port) and continuing until the lighthouse at Point Lynas comes into view (*below*).

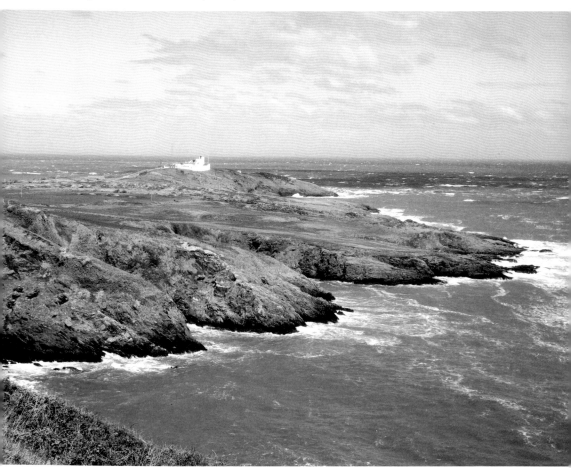

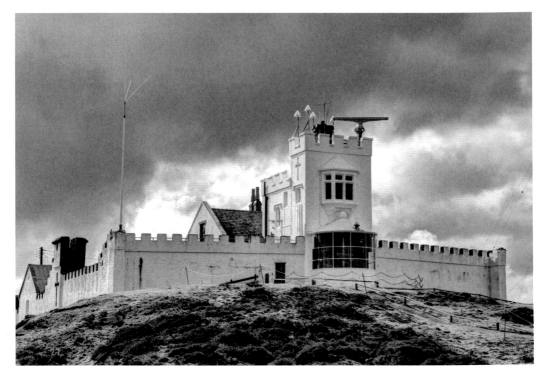

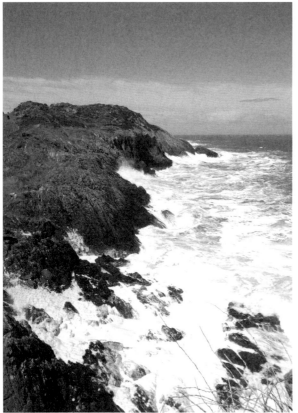

The Point Lynas lighthouse (*above*) was built by the Mersey Docks & Harbour Board in 1835, although there were lights on this rocky peninsula from the late 1700s. The lighthouse tower unusually has the lantern at its base and is now fully automated. The distinctive castellated building includes a number of restored lighthouse keepers' cottages, which are now used for private and holiday accommodation. A great spot to 'get away from it all'!

Our route crosses the neck of the Point Lynas peninsula, turning left on the lighthouse access lane then following the lane around Porth Eilian, continuing through a little gate on the right. There's a great view from the ongoing path looking back over Porth Eilian to the lighthouse. We continue around Porthyrychen to Porthnewydd and we can enjoy the wildness of the coast as we approach Amlwch Port. A strong onshore wind can bring the breakers crashing in (*left*).

The path swings around past a cottage heading down towards Amlwch Port and an old windmill tower can be seen on the headland opposite. The path reaches a parking area then, just past a little stack, goes right, down some steps by the Sail Loft Visitor Centre.

The Sail Loft Centre is an excellent place to visit and has an informative exhibition about the history of Amlwch Port, including its copper trade, shipbuilding, brewing and tobacco industries. The display also tells some fascinating tales about the prominent characters who played their part in the story of Amlwch. The building itself was once part of Captain William Thomas's shipyard and still has the sloping floor where large pieces of canvas sailcloth were stitched together to make the sails for Amlwch ships. A welcoming café and gift shop complete the experience.

We emerge at the harbour of Amlwch Port to walk along the quay where the Copper Kingdom Centre is another award-winning heritage facility. The interactive displays tell the story of how copper was mined at Parys Mountain and brought down to Amlwch Port to be processed and exported around the world. The days when Anglesey was the world's leading copper producer can certainly be relived here. Both centres are open at Easter and from Whitsun to October.

Amlwch was a tiny fishing port before copper was discovered but it developed rapidly in the late eighteenth century as the copper boom accelerated. Its harbour is formed by a narrow natural creek with steep rocks on either side, and although it was only about 100 feet wide at its entrance, it had to be protected from the savage northerly winds. The print below shows the entrance to Amlwch Harbour in 1815, with many sailing ships in the port. The copper bins on the quayside are near where the Copper Kingdom Centre is located today.

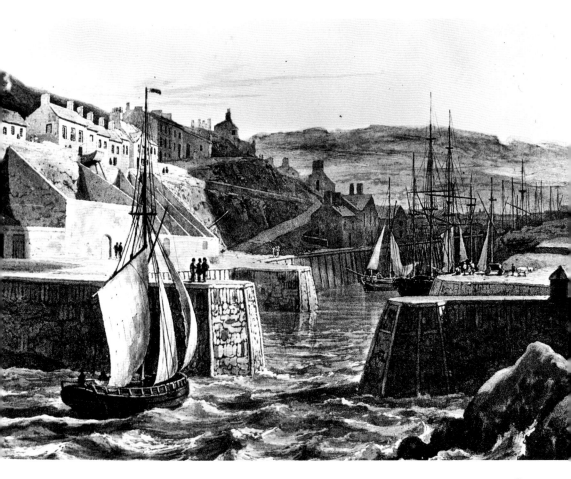

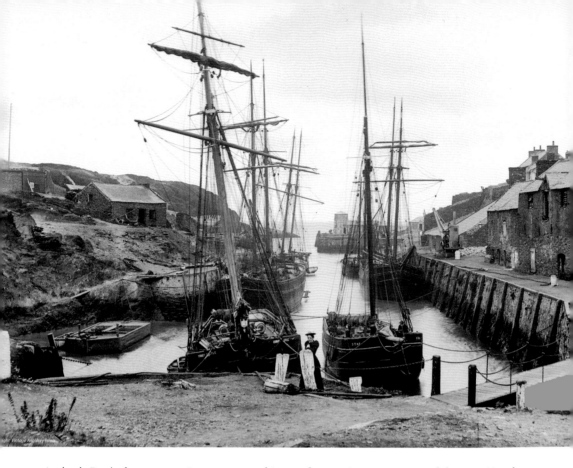

Amlwch Port's days as a major copper smelting and exporting centre started from 1768, when rich deposits of copper were discovered at nearby Parys Mountain. The trade continued up to the 1850s, by which time the copper industry was in decline. During that period, it was one of the most important ports in Wales, transporting copper ore in vast quantities to South Wales and Merseyside. It also exported corn and other agricultural produce, while imports included general goods and coal for the smelters.

The scene at the port was still vibrant in the 1850s, as recorded by Robert Roberts, 'Y Sgolor Mawr' (The Great Scholar), who described it as 'a busy port, full of ships, and the smell of sulphuric smoke from the smelting works; numerous public houses around the port, and seamen, shipwrights and hobblers drinking Amlwch Brewery beer, and chewing Amlwch shag tobacco and at least seven pugilistic encounters in the street between old Mrs. Roos' pub and Roberts' lodging house.'

Shipbuilding became the main industry in the mid-1850s with prosperous shipyards on both sides of the port engaged in building and repairing ships. The wooden and iron sailing ships and small steamers built in Amlwch were highly praised and included the three-masted schooner *Cymric*, built in the yard of Captain William Thomas in 1893. The *Cymric* was later used as a heavily armed decoy Q-ship during the First World War. Amlwch vessels operated all over the world and the days of sail are nicely illustrated in the photograph above, taken at Amlwch Port in 1895.

Our day's walk ends at the slipway at the end of the quay. Amlwch town centre is about half a mile distant and may be visited by turning right at the end of Quay Street and walking up the hill.

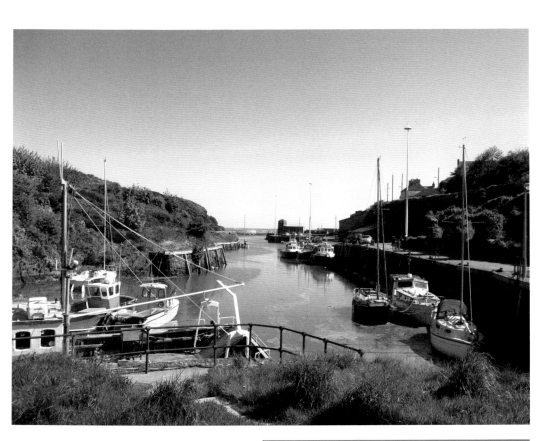

Amlwch Port today is less frenetic than it was but still conveys a sense of history (*above*). The Watch House near the harbour entrance still stands and this was where the 'hobblers' gathered; it was their job to manoeuvre ships in and out of the port.

The Amlwch Brewery Company was established at the port in 1780 and its water was drawn from St Eleth's Well, said to have magical and curative properties. It was the beer that did the trick for many, however, and by the end of the nineteenth century there were reputedly over seventy inns and beerhouses in Amlwch. A glance at the 1889 Ordnance Survey map shows numerous taverns clustered around the port, including the Packet House, Newhaven, Ship & Castle, Blue Bell, Adelphi Vaults, Liverpool Arms, Eagle Inn, Royal Oak and Watermans Arms. Few of these remain, but happily the Adelphi Vaults (*right*) is still flying the flag near the quayside.

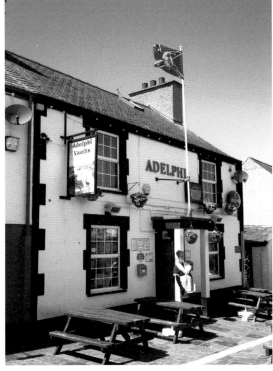

Chapter Ten
Amlwch Port to Cemaes Bay
8.0 miles (12.8 km)

The Journey's End

Today we leave Amlwch, the northernmost town in Wales, and visit some other 'northernmost' places on our way to Cemaes Bay. The walk takes us along some of the most breathtaking coastline in Wales and there are a number of steep ascents and descents along the way. We visit Bull Bay then continue to the lovely bay of Porth Wen, with its old brickworks and sea arch. After dropping steeply down into Porth Cynfor (Hell's Mouth), we climb up to Llanlleiana Head and its lookout tower. We then continue to Cemaes Bay and take a little boat trip to see the actual northernmost point in Wales at Middle Mouse island.

We can't leave Amlwch, however, without visiting Parys Mountain, the heart of 'Copper Kingdom'. This is a separate 6.6-mile circular walk following the Copper Coast Heritage Trail, the route of which is marked on the map opposite. The circular walk is not described here but some information and images of Parys Mountain are included.

Parys Mountain is sometimes called the 'Great Opencast' and looking out at the scene from the site's viewing point (*below*), it's easy to understand why.

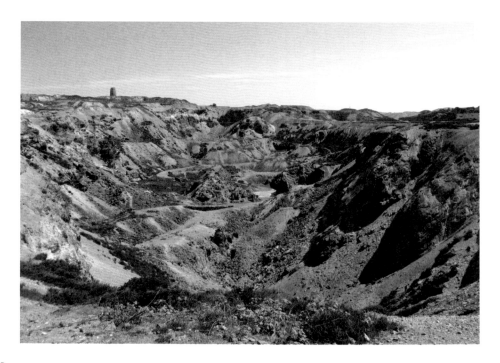

Copper mining at Parys Mountain probably dates from the Bronze Age and the striking colours of the various mineral deposits can still be seen in the incredible landscape. The Romans were active on the mountain but the 'great discovery' took place in 1768, when vast amounts of copper were found near the surface. Roland Puw, a local miner who was present at the discovery, was rewarded with a bottle of brandy and a rent-free cottage for life.

The exploitation of the huge copper reserves was known as the 'Golden Venture' and under the management of Anglesey lawyer, Thomas Williams, Parys Mountain became the world's most important copper mine. He took control of the two mines on the mountain, the Mona and the Parys, settling disputes between them and becoming known as Twm Chwarae Teg (Tom Fair Play). He was widely regarded as the 'Copper King' as Parys Mountain became one of the largest opencast mines in the world, employing over 1,200 people at its peak.

It's difficult to comprehend that the gigantic chasm was largely created by manual labour, using picks and shovels and gunpowder. Mining was a hazardous occupation, with miners perilously suspended on ropes, hacking away at the rock faces. The copper ore was broken up by 'Copper Ladies' and children using hammers to separate out the richer pieces.

The circular walk around the site passes the Pearl Engine House, which pumped water out of the mine. The summit windmill (*right*) was used to supplement the pumping. The walk also passes numerous precipitation ponds where pure copper was obtained from drainage water, using scrap iron in the ponds.

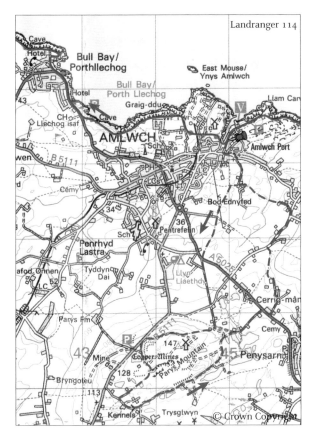

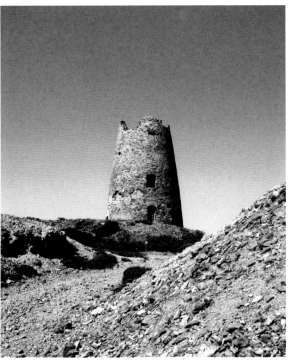

From Amlwch Port we cross the slipway and bear right on the Coastal Path, passing around the back of the harbour and over a footbridge. The path bears left to join a track where we turn left, passing through a car park and across a playing field. The path then turns left alongside the Afon Goch stream to reach the road, which we cross to a gate on the other side. We cross an old railway line to reach a kissing gate, turning right to continue ahead to the coast then turning left on the Coastal Path with East Mouse island offshore. The path reaches the road just before Bull Bay, near the cove of Pwll y Tarw (Bull Pool), which gives the village its English name. The village is the northernmost in Wales and its Welsh name, Porthllechog, means 'sheltered bay', for which generations of sailors have been grateful.

A safe haven was not to be found for the SS *Dakota*, which was wrecked on the night of 9 May 1877. She left Liverpool bound for New York carrying 218 passengers and 109 crew together with a substantial cargo. The weather was calm but due to a catastrophic navigational error, she was grounded on rocks inshore of East Mouse. All those on board were rescued, thanks in no small part to the efforts of the Bull Bay lifeboat crew. The ship broke in two the following day, becoming a wreck that has since been a favoured site for divers. The lifeboat at Bull Bay was withdrawn in the 1920s.

We turn right at the road, passing the Trecastell Hotel to go down to the village. The photograph below shows the road passing Glan Dŵr Farm in 1911 with the Bull Bay Hotel overlooking the bay. Our path turns right by the Bull Bay Hotel, going up some steps and then turning right to follow the Coastal Path around the headland.

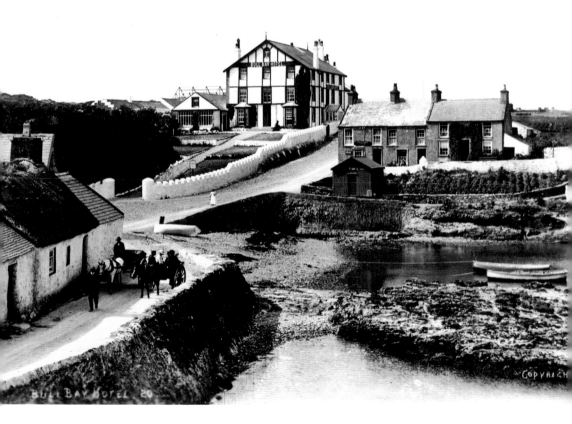

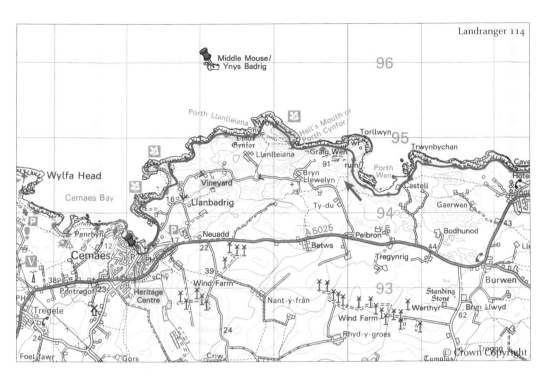

The route follows the coast edge, passing around an inlet and continuing ahead on the Coastal Path to round the headland of Trwynbychan and reach the magnificent bay of Porth Wen, where there's a great view across to an old abandoned brickworks (*below*).

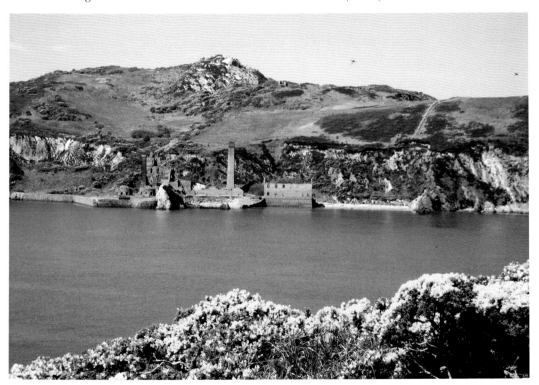

The path passes behind Castell farmhouse, continuing around the back of Porth Wen Bay and above the brickworks ruins. It's amazing to find the old chimney stacks and 'beehive' kilns in this remote location. The brickworks used local clay and quartzite that was mined from rocky outcrops nearby to manufacture special silica bricks for the steel industry. Mining here probably started around 1850, but the brickworks buildings date from about 1900. They produced good quality bricks and tiles, but everything had to be brought in and out by sea, using the little quay alongside. This was quite a difficult operation, subject to the vagaries of the tides and the heavy swell from northerly winds. Production here ended at the outbreak of the Second World War and very little was done thereafter.

The Coastal Path forks left below Torllwyn, but a walk up to the mast is rewarded with a good view of the brickworks and Porth Wen Bay's beautifully formed rock arch. Returning to the path, we pass an old winch house, which may have been used to lower the quartzite rock down to the brickworks. Soon we see Llanlleiana Head and its lookout tower, but first the path drops steeply down to the rocky inlet of Porth Cynfor (Hell's Mouth). Care is needed here as the path goes very near the cliff edge in places. A steep climb takes us up to Llanlleiana Head, which is the second most northerly point in Wales – the northernmost is Middle Mouse island, which we can see offshore. The ruined lookout tower (*below*) shares the headland with an Iron Age hill fort known as Dinas Gynfor.

From Llanlleiana Head, the path zig-zags steeply down into Porth Llanlleiana, where there are the remains of a porcelain works with a chimney bizarrely protruding from the hillside (*opposite above*).

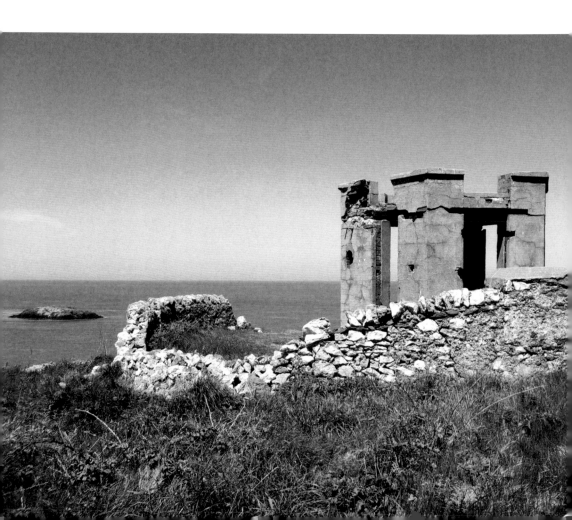

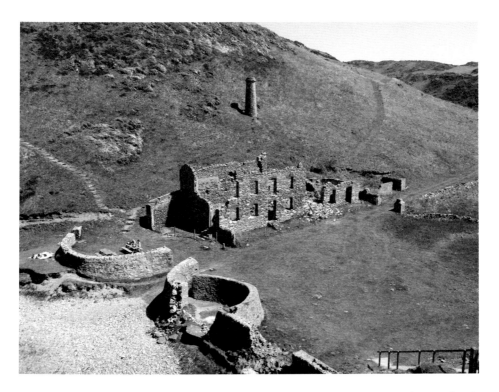

From Porth Llanlleiana we climb steep steps and follow the well-waymarked Coastal Path as it continues to St Padrig's church (*below*). This is the only church in Wales dedicated directly to St Patrick of Ireland; legend says he was shipwrecked on the island before finding refuge in a nearby cave.

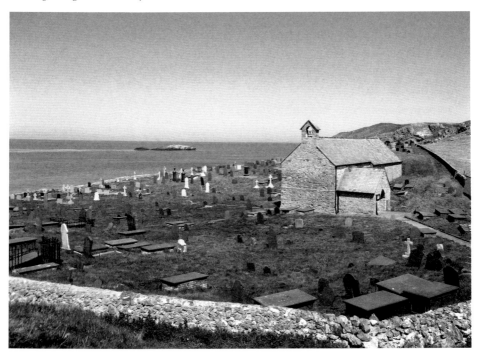

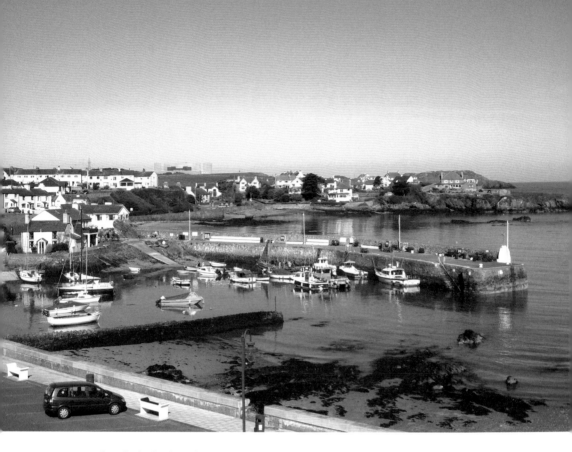

Having explored Llanbadrig church, we go down the lane before turning right to walk around the back of the delightful little cove of Porth Padrig. We pass an old limekiln, a reminder of times past, and continue around the headland of Trwyn y Parc to finally reach the bay of Cemaes. A walk along the promenade at the back of the beach takes us to the attractive harbour (*above*). Nearby is the centre of the village, where there are several excellent places of refreshment. We've reached the end of our long walk through Wales and Cemaes Bay is the perfect place to celebrate our journey's end. A little boat trip to Middle Mouse island is all that remains.

The village of Cemaes Bay vies with Bull Bay as the most northerly in Wales and has been a fishing village since ancient times. Its main connection with the outside world has always been the sea and in the eighteenth and nineteenth centuries, Cemaes became a thriving port. Exports included limestone and marble from nearby White Lady Bay as well as corn and lime from the kilns. Cemaes developed a shipbuilding industry in the 1830s and ships of up to 400 tons were built in the harbour. Later on, bricks from the local brickworks were exported, with a tramway delivering the bricks to the harbour and conveying imported coal to fire the kilns. The coming of the roads and railways saw the gradual decline of the port, but the bay's beauty and outstanding location has continued to attract many visitors. Cemaes Bay remains a popular holiday resort and is one of the pearls of the north Anglesey coast.

Cemaes Bay also provides some interesting contrasts regarding energy sources. It has wind turbines on one side of the village and the Wylfa nuclear station on the other.

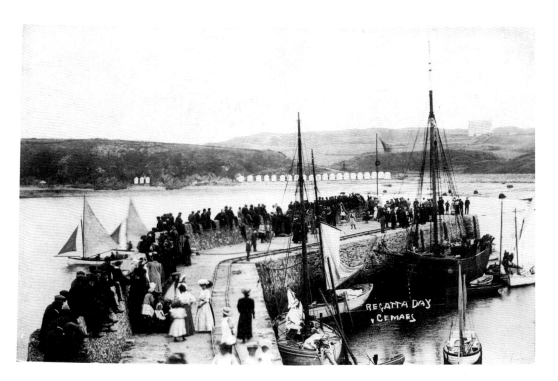

It is interesting to look at images from Cemaes Bay's past. The photograph above shows the Cemaes Regatta in 1909, a popular event attracting the crowds in their Edwardian dress. The harbour wall clearly provided a good vantage point for watching the yacht races.

The image below shows the 'Alma' bus outside the Olde Vigour Inn in 1913. The bus may have been named in honour of the battle in which the bus owner's father had fought. The Stag Hotel is also shown – perhaps the sailor we can see had just left the pub.

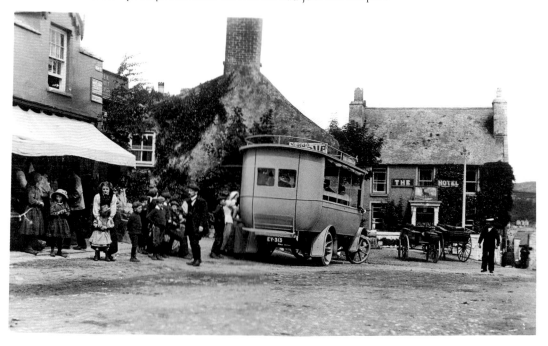

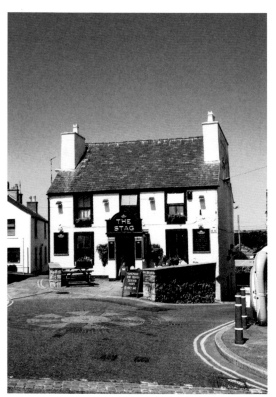

The Stag at Cemaes Bay *(left)* is the northernmost pub in Wales and a good place to relax and reflect at the end of a remarkable walk through time. The journey has been truly exceptional, from the southernmost point at Flat Holm Island to Cardiff Bay and the South Wales valleys; the Brecon Beacons and the valley of the Wye; Glyndŵr's ancient capital and the ascents of Cadair Idris and Snowdon; the great castles, including Caerphilly and Caernarfon, and some of the most breathtaking coastline imaginable. The list of highlights is endless.

But still we haven't finished. A boat trip to Middle Mouse island aboard *Stingray* with Dafydd Williams at the helm provides the icing on the cake. The island is also known as Ynys Badrig (Patrick's island), where legend says St Patrick was shipwrecked. To encircle the island *(below)* and witness countless guillemots nesting at Wales's northernmost point is the perfect ending.

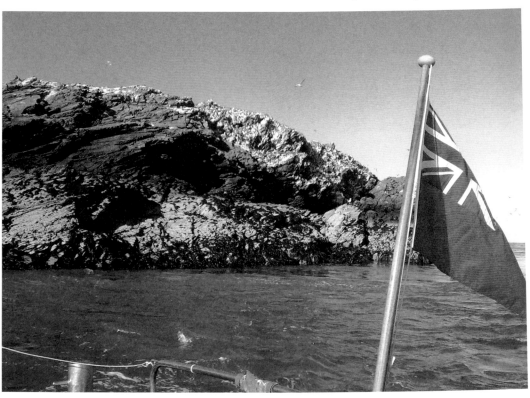